The Living Well Guide for
SENIOR DOGS

Everything You Need to Know for a Happy & Healthy Companion

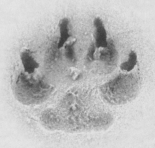

DIANE MORGAN

WAYNE HUNTHAUSEN, D.V.M.,
CONSULTING VETERINARY EDITOR

The Living Well Guide for Senior Dogs

Project Team
Editor: Stephanie Fornino
Copy Editor: Ellen Bingham
Indexer: Joann Woy
Designer: Stephanie Krautheim

T.F.H. Publications
President/CEO: Glen S. Axelrod
Executive Vice President: Mark E. Johnson
Publisher: Christopher T. Reggio
Production Manager: Kathy Bontz

T.F.H. Publications, Inc.
One TFH Plaza
Third and Union Avenues
Neptune City, NJ 07753

Printed and bound in China

07 08 09 10 11   1 3 5 7 9 8 6 4 2

Library of Congress Cataloging-in-Publication Data

Morgan, Diane, 1947-
  The living well guide for senior dogs : everything you need to know for a happy & healthy companion / Diane Morgan.
     p. cm.
  Includes index.
  ISBN 978-0-7938-0618-8 (alk. paper)
  1. Dogs. 2. Dogs–Aging. 3. Dogs–Health. 4. Dogs–Nutrition. 5. Dogs–Diseases. I. Title.

SF427.M7454 2007
636.7'08930438–dc22
                                        2007017526

This book has been published with the intent to provide accurate and authoritative information in regard to the subject matter within. While every reasonable precaution has been taken in preparation of this book, the author and publisher expressly disclaim responsibility for any errors, omissions, or adverse effects arising from the use or application of the information contained herein. The techniques and suggestions are used at the reader's discretion and are not to be considered a substitute for veterinary care. If you suspect a medical problem, consult your veterinarian.

The Leader In Responsible Animal Care For Over 50 Years!®
www.tfh.com

CENTRAL
Garden & Pet

Contents

❦ *Introduction* ❧

"Blessed is the person who has earned the love of an old dog."
—*Sydney Jeanne Seward*

How did it happen? Your cute, bouncing nine-week-old puppy has disappeared into the mists of time. Gone forever is the youthful bark, the scampering steps, the joyful tearing around the house. Thank goodness!

Your precious but aggravating puppy has slowly matured into a dignified, well-behaved, sensible senior citizen. You no longer have to tape electrical cords to the wall and hide the toilet paper. You don't have to run your legs off trying to give him enough exercise to tire him out. You don't have to take him out six times a day to try to get him to pee, only to find out that he prefers to use the Oriental rug. Your little puppy has transformed into a responsible senior citizen who is no longer traumatized by bicycles and stunned into a frenzy of barking by the letter carrier. He has become a responsible senior who knows and understands the world around him.

If you've been smart enough to skip the puppy stage altogether and adopt your dog as a senior, congratulations. You've chosen to enrich your life with a wise friend who knows the value of a comfortable home and the pleasures of lounging before the fire without the desire to stick his head into it. Adding an older dog to a home is like inviting in an old friend.

While owning a senior has its special set of challenges, the rewards are immeasurable. Senior dogs teach us to honor age and dignity. They show us how the end of life can be as interesting and rewarding as the beginning and that there's always something new to learn. In addition, if you have raised your dog from the time he was a puppy, he finally understands you—he knows your routines, your character, and your tiny little temperament flaws.

So congratulations on owning a senior dog. You have distinguished yourself as a dog owner by keeping your puppy alive and healthy into his golden years, and he will reward you to his very last minute on earth.

This book will help you and your older dog make the most of his golden years by considering such important facets of senior life as diet, grooming, activities, and health care. While these things are important to all dogs, seniors deserve special attention and pampering. They certainly earned it!

≪ *Chapter 1* ≫

SENIOR DOGS 101

Dogs are so much like people that it's scary. And part of the similarity is in the way we age. Like people, dogs slow down, stiffen up, go gray, mellow out, and stop acting like silly kids. But the rate at which all this happens varies wildly from individual to individual, as well as between breeds.

There

$There$ are no specific demarcation lines between puppyhood, adulthood, and senior status (even if you do celebrate your dog's birthday). One day melts into another, and there's always that shock when you notice the first gray hair or the first slight stiffness in the morning.

IS MY DOG A SENIOR?

The average life span of the North American or European dog is 12.8 years, an average that has gone up greatly in the past 100 years because of the availability of better food and better vet care. In general, the rate of aging and the projected life span of dogs are size-dependent. As a rule, smaller dogs live longer than medium-sized ones, who live longer than large ones, who live longer than giant breeds. (See chart.)

Weight of Dog	Breed Examples	Age at Which Dog Considered a Senior
15 pounds (6.8 kg) and smaller	Chihuahua, Maltese, Pomeranian, Toy Poodle, Yorkshire Terrier	11
Between 16 and 50 pounds (7.3 and 22.7 kg)	Border Collie, Beagle, Corgi, Cocker Spaniel, Dachshund	9
Between 51 and 80 pounds (23.1 and 36.3 kg)	Boxer, Golden Retriever, Greyhound, Labrador Retriever, Standard Schnauzer	8
More than 80 pounds (36.3 kg)	Bullmastiff, Great Dane, Irish Wolfhound, Mastiff, Newfoundland	6

However, there also seems to be a difference in breeds, which may be independent, to some degree, of size. Every once in a while someone draws up a chart comparing dogs of different breeds to a corresponding age in human beings. One such chart, a

Adopting a Senior Dog

If you are thinking about adopting a dog, please consider giving a senior dog a chance. Puppies are adorable and are snatched up quickly, but many seniors wait out lonely weeks hoping to be adopted before finally being euthanized. This is such a tragedy.

People who have adopted senior dogs will tell you what wonderful pets they make, especially if you have a busy lifestyle that can't accommodate the incessant demands of a puppy. Their calm demeanor makes them more tolerant of children (and much less apt to nip) than puppies. They are much less likely to jump all over you, which is a big advantage for large-breed dogs, nor are they likely to drag you all around the neighborhood in a mad urge to explore every tree, other person, and gutter. Best of all, many older dogs come already trained, both in the housetraining and obedience department—a huge plus.

If you have already adopted a senior—hats off! You have not only made a reasonable and responsible choice, but you have performed a very kind act.

regression analysis of 117 breeds, is so precise that it lists a 10-year-old Afghan as 66.1 in "human years" and a Beagle as 66.6! While this approach does give you a handle on how old your dog really is, it has its problems—at both ends. Both dogs and humans age at different rates. Some 66-year-old humans are running marathons; others are in nursing homes. The same is true of dogs. Your dog will age at his own pace, but the good news is that your quality care can keep him young much longer than many charts indicate.

THE AGING PROCESS

Just as with people, bodily processes change as dogs age. This doesn't mean that they become decrepit—"older" can mean "better" well into old age. However, aging is a tricky business. Differences in appearance and behavior develop that you must observe and make necessary allowances for.

Most older dogs experience some sensory, system, or psychological changes, or a combination of the three. (For more information on specific diseases that affect seniors, see Chapter 7.) You probably will not even notice some of these changes, especially if they are gradual, because dogs are remarkably good at covering up their disabilities and compensating for them. This is because in the wild, sick dogs are perceived as weak and are more likely to be targeted by a predator. No dog wants to be the target of an attack, so it makes sense to pretend that all is well, even when it isn't. Although your senior dog isn't living in the wild, his natural instincts warn him that it's still best to cover up signs of sickness.

In general, the rate of aging and the projected life span of dogs are size-dependent. A small dog like the Pomeranian may be considered a senior at 11 years; a Beagle at 9 years; a Boxer at 8 years; and a Great Dane at 6 years.

While aging is inevitable, many of its more unfortunate side effects are not. Let's take a look at the some of the normal changes that occur in any creature of distinguished age—human or canine.

Sensory Changes

While it's obvious to owners that their seniors dogs have slowed down a bit, it's important to remember that subtler but equally important changes are at work in the sensory department.

Ears and Hearing

As dogs and people age, the nerve cells and other parts of the hearing apparatus degenerate, and the eardrum loses its ability to respond easily to vibrations; both processes result in hearing loss. Ear infections also become more common.

Because the inner ear is responsible for providing a sense of balance, older dogs may get tottery for reasons that have nothing to do with their shakier legs. In fact, problems with balance are sometimes misdiagnosed as hind limb weakness.

On the other hand, don't simply assume that poor hearing is inevitably the result of old age. Infections, abnormal growths, or foreign bodies, all of which can occur at any age, also may be responsible.

Eyes and Vision

For most beings, eyesight diminishes with age, and it is common for eyes to become somewhat drier with the passing years. Regular exposure to ultraviolet light over the life of a dog is damaging to the eye lens, and over time, it will become cloudy.

As they get older, many dogs develop a hardening in the lens of the eye. This causes the lens to become slightly opaque and bluish in the center region. This process is called nuclear sclerosis and becomes noticeable in dogs around eight to ten years of age.

Often, the pupil cannot expand and contract to the same degree as when they were younger, so senior dogs have more trouble seeing both in the dark and in very bright light. This is normal and doesn't mean much, if any, vision loss.

Certain eye conditions, like glaucoma and cataracts, are more frequent in senior dogs. Glaucoma is more common in older dogs because the eye's aqueous humor (a clear fluid in the eye) may not drain as effectively as before, resulting in increased internal pressures and eventually glaucoma and blindness.

If calcium deposits form on the cornea, corneal disease may occur, resulting in extreme photophobia (intolerance of light). Dogs, however, do not depend on sight as much as people do, and blind dogs adjust to their environment quite well.

Nose and Smell

Even the dog's celebrated sense of smell takes a beating in extreme old age. After the age of 14, degenerative changes occur. By the time a dog reaches the age of 17, these changes are very noticeable. In addition, because various tumors and polyps become increasingly common in older dogs, they may resort to mouth breathing, which adversely affects their smelling ability.

Tongue and Taste

It is very difficult to test for taste because the sense of smell is so intimately bound up with that of taste. (If you hold your breath, it's really hard to tell if you are biting into an apple or an onion.) However, we do know that human beings lose taste buds as they age, so we can assume that the same is probably true of dogs, who don't have as many as humans do to begin with. Some of these taste buds are located back in the throat, by the way, so a dog doesn't really "taste" the food until he is actually swallowing it. Considering some of the stuff they eat, that's probably a good thing!

System Changes

The senses aren't alone in feeling the effects of old

SENIOR TALES

"Ruby"

Diane says, "When my senior Basset Hound, Ruby, started to show signs of age, I remember feeling sad—until I stopped to think about it. Ruby didn't care that her muzzle was gray because she couldn't see it anyway. She didn't mind that she could no longer run several blocks, either; a moderate walk was just as interesting to her as her former hour-long romps had been. Ruby taught me that the golden years can indeed be golden, as well as deeply appreciated."

age. The rest of the bodily systems also slow down.

Cardiovascular System: The Pumphouse

As a dog ages, his cardiovascular system becomes less effective. Bone marrow becomes more fatty and less functional, producing fewer red blood cells and slowly leading to anemia. Fortunately, dogs of any age almost never suffer from heart attacks. Much more common are heart disturbances, an enlarged heart, and valve closure defects, producing what is called a "heart murmur," caused by scarring or loss of elasticity. Degenerating heart valves and heart muscles serve to reduce cardiac output by about one third during the last third of a dog's life, leading to a lower level of activity in older dogs.

Digestive System: The Fuel Factory

As a dog ages, the lining of the stomach begins to deteriorate. This can add up to more digestive problems of all sorts, including vomiting, diarrhea, and loss of appetite. In addition, the pancreas of an older dog may not secrete enough digestive enzymes to fully digest his food. So sometimes, even if you have your dog on a highly nutritious diet, the food doesn't get broken down properly and assimilated. Food may just zip unchanged through the intestinal tract and then become passed in the feces. This is called malabsorption.

Like humans, dogs may lose taste buds as they age.

The old colon just doesn't work the way it used to, either. Older dogs who don't get enough water and exercise may suffer from constipation and even colon impaction. If a dog is often constipated, he may develop a rectal prolapse from frequent straining. Older dogs are also more likely to develop chronic anal sac disease. Colitis is a common old-age problem in dogs, often originating from recurring bouts with intestinal parasites, like whipworms and hookworms. Very old dogs also have more trouble absorbing calcium from the small intestine, making this critical mineral less available to the blood and organs.

Metabolism is simply a way of referring to the chemical reactions that occur within the body. As we age, these reactions slow down. (Blame the thyroid gland—it's responsible for a lot of metabolism, but as it ages, it just doesn't work as well as it used to.) As the metabolic rate of older dogs slows down, that comfortable middle-aged paunch appears, along with a desire to remain more sedentary. Compared to a young dog, an older one may show a 30 percent decrease in metabolic rate. Older dogs actually need 30 to 40 percent fewer calories than young adults to maintain a svelte figure.

Endocrine System: The Hormone Factory
Most dogs show some loss of thyroid function as they age. Consequently, older dogs are subject to a wide range of immune-mediated diseases. They are also more prone to developing diabetes and Cushing's syndrome. Both are serious conditions, but both are treatable.

Immune System Function: Fighting Disease
The immune system of older dogs is weaker, and infections become more common and dangerous. The thymus gland grows smaller, too. This gland is most active early in life, where it plays an important role in cell-mediated immunity by producing T-cells. It shrinks in older animals, which lessens their immune-producing abilities.

Throughout the life of a dog, a process called peroxidation occurs in which the body destroys old, damaged cells and also kills germs and parasites. However, peroxidation is a scattergun approach that destroys healthy cells as well as sick ones. As your dog gets older, the damage caused by peroxidation accumulates and in turn increases the risk of certain problems such as infections.

Integumentary System: Skin and Coat
The skin and coats of older dogs lose some of their pliability as the oil-producing sebaceous glands become less functional. Most dogs develop a white or gray muzzle, a sign of great distinction. The coat looks dull and feels harsher than before. Many dogs lose some hair because the hair cells lose their ability to regenerate, and hair follicles become less

An older dog's metabolism slows down, making him prone to weight gain.

active. The paw pads begin to thicken, and the nails become thicker and more brittle, making them harder to trim.

In addition, wounds heal more slowly, skin responses to allergies worsen, and various skin problems emerge, like lipomas (fatty tissue tumors), cysts, and warts. The skin thickens and darkens in senior dogs. Skin tumors of all types become more common in both male and female dogs. In male dogs, the prepuce (foreskin of the penis) becomes more pendulous as the skin loses its elasticity.

Muscular System: The Powerhouse

The muscles of older dogs have less myoglobin, the hemoglobin-like protein found in muscle tissue that makes muscles look red. This protein also allows muscles to store the oxygen needed for muscle contraction. Reduced myoglobin means reduced cardiovascular capacity, lower maximum heart rate, and exercise intolerance.

As your dog grows older, there is a decrease in body mass and muscle tissue, although some pets gain total body mass because of fat storage. Mild loss of muscle mass, especially in the hind legs, may occur with old age. The dog seems to "shrink" a little. In addition, connective tissue becomes increasingly stiff. This affects not only the muscles but also makes the organs, blood vessels, and airways more rigid.

Myasthemia gravis, an autoimmune disease that interferes with the transmission of nerve impulses to muscle cells, is more common in old age. Older dogs are also subject to progressive myopathy. Both diseases manifest themselves as general weakness.

Nervous System: The Command Center

As the brain ages, it experiences a loss of neurons, and the brain cells atrophy. This kind of genetically programmed brain cell death is called "brain cell apoptosis."

In addition, there is increased B-amyloid (a plaque-forming peptide) deposition, which disrupts cognitive ability and releases more free radicals. A free radical is simply a molecule with an unpaired electron. (Remember your high school chemistry?) That doesn't sound so bad, but believe me, free radicals can play havoc with your cells in a process called oxidation. Oxidative damage to proteins and lipids also occurs, which disrupts cellular function both in the brain and all over the body.

To understand this a little better, we need to know about mitochondria. Forget chemistry and get out the biology book. Mitochondria are bean-like structures inside the cell that produce energy to power the cell. However, the by-products of their work are these highly toxic free radicals. As the brain ages, the mitochondria become less efficient, producing less energy and more free radicals, which can lead to reduced brain function and behavior changes. Antioxidant supplements such as vitamin E may slow the loss of brain function.

Tissues of the nervous system, including the brain, are especially vulnerable to attack by free radicals. One reason for this is that free radicals love to go after fatty tissue, which is a major component of the brain.

The glucose utilization rate of the cerebral cortex drops by almost half between youth and old age. The brain also has an extremely high demand for oxygen but little natural antioxidant defense and repair capabilities. (For reasons not completely understood, male dogs seem more at risk from free radical attack than females.) Also, as the brain loses neural cells, there is a corresponding loss of all sensory perception: sight, smell, hearing, and taste.

⤠ Senior Moment ⤠

Brain Changes

Because of changes in the brain, old dogs experience such problems as sleep disorders and behavioral changes like separation anxiety, loss of housetraining, barking, and shyness. Fortunately, these things are treatable. (For more information, see Chapter 5.)

Renal System: Toxic Removal

The whole renal system begins to fail as dogs get older. Old bladders just don't work as well as young ones. Older dogs also tend to have more wastes in their blood because of decreased kidney function. Both kidney function and control over the urinary bladder sphincter weakens, producing a leaky dog. Unneutered (castrated) males, due to an enlarged prostate gland and constriction of the urethra, often strain to urinate, and unneutered (spayed) older females often have a problem with incontinence. Older dogs are also prone to bladder stones.

Reproductive System: The Source of Life

Hopefully your old dog is neutered. Testicular tumors are the second most common tumor of intact male dogs, especially males with undescended testicles, who are about 14 times more likely to develop this form of cancer. Unneutered male dogs often develop infections in or tumors of the prostate gland. One study found that 60 percent of all male dogs over eight years of age have an enlarged prostate.

Unspayed females or females spayed after their first heat cycle are at a higher risk of mammary tumors. In females, the second most common form of cancer associated with aging is breast cancer, second only to various skin cancers. However,

Grayness around the muzzle is one telltale sign of aging.

mammary cancer in dogs is not as serious as in human beings, and only about half of mammary tumors are malignant. Even in cases where a malignancy exists, the cancer is not as aggressive as with people, and surgery usually stops the cancer in its tracks. The unspayed female is also subject to pyometra, a deadly uterine infection.

Respiratory System: The Breath of Life

Older dogs lose elasticity in the lungs, and the volume of the lungs decreases, reducing lung capacity. This means that seniors tolerate exercise less, as well as tire and run out of breath easily.

Skeletal System: The Bare Bones

Older dogs have less cartilage, so their old bones start scraping against each other, causing arthritis. Canine hip dysplasia, if present from an early age, will be exacerbated in old age, leading to arthritis. Bones need to be stressed to maintain their calcification, and in older dogs with reduced exercise, bone density decreases, and the bones fracture more easily.

Your senior dog deserves some extra care and attention.

Psychological Changes

Minds, like bodies, change with the years. In many ways, this is a good thing. Older dogs are not as distractible as puppies. If they are slower to learn new tricks, they are also unlikely to pick up any more bad habits. And while some dogs do seem to get a little "senile" with the passing years, most dogs remain their former selves, just with more dignity.

Contrary to popular belief, the healthy aging dog does not undergo a sudden change in personality. A previously friendly dog does not become shy or vicious. A strong, self-willed dog does not turn into a shrinking violet. Dogs who did not like outsiders as puppies probably still will dislike them. Most senior dogs simply seem to become "more themselves" as they reach their golden years.

If your senior dog does seem to be turning into someone you don't know, he may be suffering from canine cognitive disorder, a treatable problem that affects behavior and which can be treated. A changed sleeping pattern, withdrawal of affection, unmotivated barking, and confusion may be signs. (For more information on this disorder, see Chapter 8.)

Older dogs may tire more easily than they did when they were younger.

If all this sounds scary, it shouldn't. Growing older is a natural part of life we all face. Our dogs can teach us to accept it with dignity and with an appreciation for the good times as they come along. Also, keep in mind that aging is almost always more of a problem for owners than it is for their dogs, who are sensible enough to accept their slowing bodies and changing lives with grace. They love their naps, their treats, and the fascinating smells wafting across the backyard. What's best, they enjoy your love, snuggles, and company more than ever.

Chapter 2

LIVING WITH YOUR SENIOR DOG

This is the twenty-first century, so there's no need to subject your senior dog to Stone Age conditions. If you want your dog to live his longest and happiest life, it's up to you to provide the equipment and environment for him to do just that.

SENIOR SUPPLIES

Older dogs deserve their own "things," just as puppies do. In many cases, these are the same items, like crates, gates, bowls, and beds. Nowadays, though, the pet trade is catering to senior dogs—an increasingly large portion of the market—and you will be able to shop to your heart's content for supplies that make your old dog happy and comfortable.

Baby Gate

Baby gates are not just for human babies. Use them to keep your older dog confined to a particular room or area of the house, either for his own protection or for that of your furniture.

Bedding

Your senior dog deserves better than an old worn-out blanket tossed on the floor for his naps. Think comfort. If you wouldn't be comfortable on that kind of bed, neither would your dog.

Older dogs have thinner bones, stiffer joints, and less muscle mass than their younger counterparts, and they need more padding. Because they also sleep more than younger dogs, their beds are very important to them. If your dog is not comfortable, he is likely to be irritable, a state of mind that won't be pleasant for either of you.

Observing your dog's sleep pattern will help you choose just the right bed. Dogs who like to curl up may enjoy a round, high-sided bed. Dogs who like to stretch out may prefer a longer bed. Many older dogs love pillows. Measure your dog when he is sleeping comfortably for the best idea of the prospective bed's ideal dimensions.

Choose a bed with a washable cover. Place the bed in a draft-free location out of the main line of traffic but close to family activities.

For his protection, use a baby gate to keep your older dog confined to a particular area of the house.

Collar and Leash

If your old dog has been wearing a choke collar all these years, now is the time to throw it away and choose a simple buckle collar or comfortable harness. His neck, which is probably a little stiff by

Buy your senior a comfortable padded bed.

now, doesn't need any more pressure on it.

If your dog is having problems getting around and needs a mobility aid, look for a front leg or rear end support harness, which will provide him with the support he needs. Models are available for both male and female dogs. For dogs with weakness in all four legs, you can select a type that goes around the middle of the dog.

Crate

Most dogs enjoy having a crate of their own. It is not only a safe den but also a necessity. Dogs who need crate rest after surgery or who must travel need to become accustomed to a crate. It is also a safe haven from noisy children and pesky younger puppies. If your dog is blind, especially newly blind,

Cleaning Up Accidents

For accidents in the house, an increasing likelihood as your pet ages, remove the waste product, then scrub the area thoroughly with warm soapy water. Use paper towels to soak up the scrubbing water. Rinse well and towel dry. When the area is completely dry, apply a deodorizer. For urine, a solution of half water and half white vinegar will neutralize the urine's ammonia. Test the solution on a hidden part of the carpet first.

A harness is a great choice for a senior dog because it doesn't put pressure on a stiff neck.

a crate is the safest place for him to relax if you can't supervise him. Keep in mind, though, that if your dog has been used to the run of the house all these years, he may not take kindly to the idea of a crate, even if he has to use one.

Crates come in several styles: wire, fiberglass, and lightweight, portable mesh. The type you select depends on your dog's preferences and the environment:

- **Wire:** A wire crate allows plenty of visibility and ventilation, a quality very important for senior dogs who have a hard time breathing. However, some shy dogs find them "too exposed," and they can be drafty.
- **Fiberglass:** A fiberglass crate is comforting and denlike, but it can overheat in the summer and fail to provide perfect ventilation for older dogs with breathing problems.
- **Mesh:** I love mesh crates because they are light and incredibly portable, but they are suitable only to dogs who enjoy being crated—a determined dog can claw his

way out of this crate.

Try to make your dog's crate as comfortable and interesting as possible by offering him an orthopedic pet bed and special treats inside it. For most dogs, that's all it takes. Never use the crate as a punishment, of course; that will just make your senior dislike being in there. Once he gets used to the idea, he'll find it's just the place to catch up on those 40 winks in peace.

Diapers

If you have an incontinent senior, you may want to consider diapers made just for dogs. These are available for both males and females, in both disposable and washable varieties. The washable kinds are usually made from a soft cotton with an absorbent liner.

Food and Water Bowls

Stainless steel water bowls, which are inexpensive, unbreakable, and easy to clean, are usually best for your dog.

Identification

Of course you recognize your dog—but if he gets lost, who else will? It's up to you to protect your old friend by making sure that he is properly ID'd.

Tags

The simplest ID is a plain dog tag with your telephone number. Attach one securely to your dog's permanent collar and keep it there. Thousands of dogs are lost and destroyed in pounds every year simply because no one knew who the animal belonged to. Visible ID tags are the best assurance that your dog will be returned.

Microchips

In addition to the traditional tag, which can, after all, fall off, consider microchipping your dog. This is a permanent invisible method of identification about the size of a grain of rice that is inserted between the shoulder blades. Unlike traditional collars and tattoos, it cannot be removed or altered. It takes only about ten seconds to microchip a dog, and the procedure is practically painless.

The microchip stores an identification number and transmits that information through radio waves to a

Your dog should have an ID tag so that he can be identified if he becomes lost.

Senior Moment

Minimize the Need for Stairs

Older dogs may fail to see stairs and fall down a flight—or may be unable to negotiate them, with the same result. Try to minimize the need for your senior dog to climb stairs by placing food and water bowls in convenient locations. Block off stairs from your senior when you are not home.

scanner. The chip is connected to a database, so you will be notified if your missing dog turns up. Currently, not all microchip scanners can read all brands of chips, but a universal standard is being developed.

Tattoos

A tattoo is another form of permanent ID. Normally a number is tattooed on your dog's groin. It can be a special number for the tattooing service or even your own telephone number (as long as you're sure that won't change!). The biggest drawback is that some tattoos become less legible over time. The tattoo should be done by a skilled pet tattooist.

Nonskid Mats and Carpet Runners

Older dogs have a harder time negotiating tile and slippery linoleum. You may want to provide nonskid mats or carpet runners on slippery surfaces. There are also sprays available for your dog's paw pads that will provide additional traction on slippery floors.

Ramps and Steps

Portable ramps or steps will help your older dog climb into a car or onto the couch. Several companies make excellent aluminum ramps with a nonskid walking surface. Some ramps telescope, with sections that slide in or out to fit long or tight spaces. Others fold up.

Older dogs with arthritis can really stiffen up while riding in the car all day long. If your old dog is too heavy or arthritic to leap into the car the way he used to, consider investing in a portable step or ramp made just for that purpose.

Toys

Although puppies are more frequent and intense chewers than older animals, all dogs enjoy an occasional chomp on a chew toy. You can select from edible snack bones, dental chews, rubber toys that hide treats, and other items. A variety of

Choose appropriately sized toys for your senior dog.

toys (rotated for interest) will help to keep your dog happy.

Squeaker toys, while tremendously popular, are troublemakers for many dogs, who destroy the toy to find and then swallow the squeaker. Be careful with rawhide chews, which may contain ingredients such as antibiotics, lead, and insecticides, depending on where they were manufactured. Safer are various types of "sustained release" balls that can be packed with treats for your dog to puzzle out.

To ensure the best results, pick a toy that is the correct size for your dog. Large dogs can choke on tennis balls, and small dogs feel overwhelmed by softballs.

SENIOR SAFETY

While your older dog isn't a silly puppy trying to get into everything, his failing sight, hearing, or locomotion may land him in a world of trouble. This section will teach you how to keep your oldster safe, an ongoing process that requires dedication and vigilance.

In the House

You may think that your home is perfectly safe. However, it is filled with medicine, a hot stove, open toilets, steep stairs, electrical wires, and other objects that can trap, poison, fall on, or choke your dog. Even old standbys like the comfortable couch can pose a danger to a geriatric dog who falls off of it.

Climate

Older dogs don't handle heat and cold extremes very well because their temperature regulation is not what it used to be. The breed itself also makes a difference. A geriatric Chihuahua can turn into an ice block at the first hint of winter, and an older Samoyed won't enjoy Florida in August. While you can't pack your dog off to Scotland in the summer and the Bahamas in January, you *can* make use of heat, air-conditioning, fans, warm or cool beds, and sweaters where appropriate.

The biggest climate-related outside danger to a dog is a car. It takes only minutes for the internal heat of a car to increase 40 degrees Fahrenheit (approximately 22 degrees Celsius) above the outside air temperature, particularly in direct sunlight. The temperature in a parked car can reach 160°F (71.1°C) in minutes, even with partially opened windows. Older dogs are much more vulnerable to overheating than young adults are.

On a hot, humid day, your older dog can become overheated, even if he's exercising only slightly and has plenty of water. Unfortunately, he has only a few methods for cooling down, none of which are very efficient. The main way is panting, which involves breathing in through the nose and out through the mouth. Panting

Caution

An old dog who pants constantly, even when he is cool, may have Cushing's disease or a respiratory problem. Consult your vet.

pulls air over the mucous membranes of the tongue to help water evaporate from it. The blood vessels on the surface of the skin also dilate to help dissipate heat. And he can sweat through the pads of his feet.

Household Poisons

What is medicine for you or cleaner to your toilets can be deadly poisons to your dog. Ordinary items like mothballs, pennies, some houseplants, coffee grounds, dough, snail bait, sugar-free candy, chocolate, and cigarettes can kill your dog if he ingests them. Always notify your vet or the ASPCA Animal Poison Control Center at (888) 426-4435 if you suspect poisoning.

The following are some common household poisons to keep out of reach of your senior.

- **Acetaminophen:** Tylenol and similar products that contain acetaminophen can damage a dog's liver and red blood cells. Signs of toxicity, such as depression, abdominal pain, vomiting, and urine that is dark in color, occur within hours. Induce vomiting by giving your dog 1 tablespoon (14.8 ml) of 3 percent hydrogen peroxide for every 10 pounds (4.5 kg) of body weight, and get your dog to a vet right away.
- **Antidepressants:** These commonly prescribed drugs are frequently left in places where dogs can get them. Depending on the amount ingested, signs of overdose include lethargy, uncoordination, vomiting, diarrhea, hyperactivity, tremors, drooling, seizures, respiratory depression, and coma. These signs can develop within 30 minutes after ingestion. Seek veterinary treatment immediately.
- **Tobacco:** Strangely enough, some dogs chew or even swallow tobacco. But it's not good for them (or for you)—in fact, nicotine is a deadly poison. Signs of nicotine poisoning include tremors, vomiting, diarrhea, and twitching or seizures. In addition, blood pressure can go dangerously high. If your dog exhibits any of these signs, take him to a vet.

Pet-Specific Weather Forecasts

Pet owners who want to be in the know consult www.weather.com/pets for pet-specific forecasts. The site tells you how to care for your dog under the forecasted conditions and gives you the best time to walk your dog. It even provides a flea population update for your area.

Smoke

Secondhand smoke is bad for pets, especially older ones. Did you know that the smoke from a cigar or cigarette contains more than 4,000 chemicals? And most of them are bad for your dog. Research shows that the chances of developing cancer are greater for dogs living in smoking environments than for dogs in nonsmoking households. Long-nosed dogs like Collies are at greatest risk because the smoke stays in their noses longer. The more smokers in the home, the higher your dog's risk of developing smoking-related cancers, lung infections, respiratory conditions, asthma, and other health problems.

Sound

Dogs have great ears; they hear frequencies that humans cannot detect and have four times the ability to distinguish pitch that humans do. Be kind to your dog's sensitive ears—he probably won't enjoy fireworks, loud music, and screaming. Any noise that makes your own ears ring is too loud for your dog and probably frightens him as well.

Your senior may benefit from a sweater or jacket in cold weather

In the Garage

You need to be as careful dog-proofing your garage as you are dog-proofing your home.

Antifreeze

The most serious danger in your garage is the antifreeze that may be dripping from your car at this very moment. Dogs are attracted to the sweet taste and often ingest lethal amounts.

The deadly ingredient in many antifreeze products is ethylene glycol. This substance is metabolized by the liver and travels through the kidneys, where it forms insoluble calcium oxalate crystals. They cause permanent damage to kidney tissue, which can ultimately lead to kidney failure. Propylene glycol antifreeze is a less toxic alternative but still is not perfectly safe. Some states are now requiring that a bitter-tasting agent be added to antifreeze to protect pets and young children.

The first signs of antifreeze toxicity are depression and lethargy; many dogs appear intoxicated. Later signs include vomiting and renal failure, followed by death three or four days later. Your vet has a test kit to detect the presence of this poison in the body. Treatment for ethylene glycol toxicity may require extended hospitalization and even then is not always successful.

Cleaning Materials

Store all cleaning materials out of your dog's reach. While older dogs don't exhibit the insatiable curiosity of puppies about these things, you can never be sure what your senior might take it into his head to experiment with. It's not worth the risk.

In the Yard

The yard is a fun place for your dog to play in and relax—it's up to you to make it safe, too.

Fleas and Ticks

If you have a problem with fleas in your area, eliminate flea habitats as much as possible. A female flea can produce 600 offspring in one month, which means that you have to act fast. They like moist, warm, shady spots filled with organic debris, so get rid of piles of straw, leaves, and grass clippings. Stack firewood away from your house. If that doesn't work, you may have to resort to a flea-killing insecticide. Follow the label instructions exactly, and allow the product to dry completely before allowing your dogs or kids into the area. Once it is dry and bound to the grass, it's safe. Most lawn

Odor Control

As some dogs age, they tend to get a little smelly—and may even lose some sphincter control. This is just a part of life, and conscientious dog owners not only do all they can to keep their pets clean and smelling good, but they also work to keep the home environment pleasant and smelling sweet.

There are many products on the market to help keep those weird stains and smells at bay. Some of the simplest are carpet powders designed to destroy pet odor (not just mask it). Be sure to wait a sufficient length of time for the powder to penetrate down into the carpet fibers. Then vacuum. Urine-saturated carpets will need more help. Choose an enzyme-activated carpet cleaner with an "odor-encapsulation formula" to rid your house of the smells of dog waste.

To keep the air clean, try an air purifier that uses an airborne electronic charge to remove dust and odors. You also can try a light ring that holds fragrant oil. As the light warms, the pleasant smell drifts through your home. For a more immediate effect, try a "fogger." This product comes in a variety of scents, any of which are nicer than canine odors.

To keep ticks away from your yard, mow the grass short and clear brush away.

treatments are safe for dogs unless you have a pet that ingests an entire bag of the stuff. A few dogs may get skin reactions from them. Some recent evidence also links lawn chemicals to cancer (lymphosarcoma) in some breeds. Your lawn is really better off *au naturel.*

Ticks are even worse than fleas, because they spread many deadly diseases, including Lyme disease and Rocky Mountain spotted fever. To keep ticks away, mow the grass short and clear brush away. If nothing else works, use a pesticide specifically labeled for ticks.

Most important, use a flea and tick preventive on your senior. New products are extremely safe for your senior pet but deadly to fleas and ticks.

Herbicides
When used as directed and allowed to dry, herbicides are fairly benign. If your dog eats a large amount of them, though, he could become poisoned or develop a

Use caution when treating your lawn with pesticides or herbicides—some dogs have reactions to them.

gastrointestinal obstruction. Dogs who are exposed to herbicides regularly are at a higher risk of developing cancer.

Metal Edging

Metal edging used to line a garden's perimeter can cause serious cuts to your dog's tender paws. It cuts right through the pads. Get rid of it or buy plastic capping to cover existing edging.

Pesticides

Pesticides like snail bait, fly bait, mole and gopher baits, rat poison, and systemic insecticides can be extremely dangerous if ingested. Keep them far away from your senior.

Poisonous Plants

Most older dogs are not interested in gobbling up amaryllis, ivy, azaleas, and daffodils, but it can happen, especially in dogs who are slightly senile and not as aware of what they are eating. And equally important, older dogs with renal or liver failure are going to be more at risk if they do transgress.

Here are some of the most commonly ingested poisonous plants—for a complete list of toxic plants, go to the ASPCA's website at www.aspca.org.

Urine Grass Stains

The truth is that older dogs urinate more than younger ones do. The good news is that because your senior urinates more frequently, the urine is less concentrated and so less harmful to grass. Still, it doesn't do it any good. If you have yellow stains from dog urine on your grass, lawn products are available to alleviate the problem. However, the simplest thing you can do is to hose down the spot after your dog urinates. That simply dilutes and washes the stuff away. It also keeps your lawn watered. If you can train your dog to urinate in the same area, of course, things will be a lot easier. But that's not always practical, especially with incontinent older dogs.

- **Autumn crocus:** Its active ingredient can cause bloody diarrhea, vomiting, and damage to the intestinal tract.
- **Azalea:** This popular ornamental bush can harm the cardiovascular system and trigger vomiting, drooling, diarrhea, and central nervous system depression.
- **Castor bean:** In this plant, the seeds contain the highest concentration of toxins, although all parts of the plant are dangerous. Ingestion can produce significant abdominal pain, vomiting, diarrhea, and weakness. Dehydration, tremors, seizures, and even death could result.
- **Lily:** Even small amounts of this flower can result in severe kidney damage.
- **Oleander:** This southern outdoor ornamental can cause hypothermia, cardiac problems, and severe irritation of the gastrointestinal tract.
- **Sago palm:** Another popular ornamental, the sago palm can produce vomiting, diarrhea, depression, seizures, liver failure, and even death.

Pools

An estimated 5,000 family pets drown in backyard swimming pools annually. Don't let yours be one of them. If you have a backyard pool, you must keep your dog out of the area when you are not there to supervise. Install a see-through pool fence and put a self-closing/locking gate on it. It's also smart to buy a floating pool-alarm device that will go off both outside and inside your home in case your dog takes an unauthorized dive.

Even if your dog has been a noted swimmer in his youth, older dogs gradually lose the ability to swim well—or at all. They also can slip more easily and fall into the pool. Once in, your family pool can become a death trap. Even barking for help becomes difficult once the dog is in the water. Unless he has been well trained to head for the stairs at the shallow end, he will simply head for the nearest edge of the pool and attempt to climb or claw his way out—an

If you have a pool, keep your senior out of the area when you are not there to supervise.

impossible task for most dogs. His panic alone will exhaust him, and he can die within seconds.

Just as dangerous as the water are the heat and unremitting sunlight around most pools. Dogs overheat easily. This is a real problem with seniors who love the water but who are no longer able to join in the swimming fun. They tend to hang around the edge of the pool, soaking up the sunlight until they are in serious danger of heatstroke.

SENIOR RELATIONSHIPS

Dogs are social creatures who are accustomed to living together in a pack. In the wild, a dog pack consists of several related animals—strangers are seldom welcomed. However, contemporary dogs are much more open-minded about these things and are often able to get along well with new people and other dogs. As a general rule, if your dog enjoyed the company of other people and dogs as a young adult, he will continue to do so.

This section will help you to help your senior dog establish a relationship with a new member of the family, including another dog, adult, or baby, and will give you tips on how to help children interact with him in the home.

With a New Dog

Perhaps now that your dog is getting on in years, you're thinking of the future. Would it be wise to get another dog, perhaps as company for your senior or perhaps to ease your own heart when the inevitable happens? An interesting question, to which the answer is a resounding "Maybe." To make the right decision, you need to ask yourself the following questions:

- **How does your dog respond to new dogs now?** If he's friendly and interested, a new dog might be a good idea. If he's a loner, though, or jealous of other dogs, it's best not to upset his declining years by importing a rival. If you're not sure, arrange for your older dog to meet with some youngsters to see how he behaves.
- **Will your older dog get the same amount of love, grooming, and attention he has now if you add a new one?** Some people are so seduced by a younger dog that the

Make sure that you give your older dog the same amount of love, grooming, and attention that you give your new dog.

older one gets shuffled off to the corner and essentially forgotten.

- **Do you have the resources in time and money to care for another dog?** Two dogs are not as easy or as inexpensive to care for as one is. While you can walk or even feed two dogs at once, they need to be groomed separately. And, of course, if they get sick (even if they both get sick at once), your vet is not likely to grant you a two-for-one fee. If one dog is stretching your budget and taking up all your free time, don't add another one.

If you can give positive answers to all these questions, you may want to consider it. A younger dog can give a senior a new lease on life. Some seniors actually seem years younger! On the other hand, a rambunctious puppy might annoy, pester, or just wear out your oldster. Choose carefully.

How to Introduce a New Dog

If you decide to bring home a new dog, don't expect your senior to be thrilled. He might be, but don't count on it. His territorial instincts may come into play, and he is bound to be a little jealous of your attentions to another dog. (Yes, dogs do get jealous. Call it territorialism or resource guarding, but it comes down to the same thing.)

The best way to ensure a smooth introduction is to let the dogs smell each other—before they set eyes on each other. When dogs first meet by visual contact, a posturing situation occurs that can lead to future stress. If possible, avoid this by first bringing home a towel or something that has the other dog's scent on it. Let your resident senior become familiar with the scent.

Set up two cages in the house. The cages should be in separate rooms out of sight from each other. Each cage will serve as a den for the dogs, providing a sense of ownership and security. Place a towel impregnated with the scent of the new dog in or near the resident dog's cage so that he becomes accustomed to the idea of the new dog. (For a dog, a smell and an idea are pretty much the same thing.) The new dog should spend his first day or so out of sight but not out of smell of the resident dog.

Then, allow your new dog freedom to explore his new home without having to deal with your old dog. (Take your oldster for a walk, or put him in another room with a great treat.) Do this several times a day. Then, switch roles; place your new dog in another room and give your senior lots of personal attention. This is critical because it will help to convince him that having a new friend around results in extra attention for himself.

When both dogs seem comfortable with each other's scent, they can meet at last. If possible, use a neutral territory, such as an enclosed dog park or even a neighbor's yard. The dogs should be unleashed unless they have displayed aggressive behavior. Leashed dogs have no "run away" option, and that can lead to the only other choice for an unhappy dog: a fight. If they are unleashed, they will be able to run, meet on their own terms, and play happily together. Then you can bring both dogs home.

With a New Adult

If it's just been the two of you for a while and then a new adult person joins the family, be prepared for some resettling. Whether the new addition is a roommate or a new spouse, your senior needs to accept that his "pack" has been expanded. Some dogs are thrilled with the idea; others are unhappy or jealous. It's important that your dog learn to listen to the

⨲ Senior Moment ⨺

Bonding Time

Get your roommate to bond with your senior dog by feeding, walking, and petting him.

If you decide to get a new puppy, make sure that he doesn't annoy or tire your senior.

commands of the new pack member. Review the commands you use with your new roommate, and ask that he or she use the same ones. Your dog may decide to test his new limits by ignoring the new person's orders. This is a time-honored ploy that many dominant canines use to see how much they can get away with. Don't fall for it.

How to Introduce a New Adult

Help your new roommate make the dog listen by using positive rewards like treats and praise for obeying. Get your roommate to bond with your dog by feeding, walking, and petting him. Soon the dog will be glad that there is an additional source of love and petting to be had.

With a New Baby

A new baby brings joy to you but possibly tragedy for the dog. Especially if this is a first baby, your dog may feel a sudden withdrawal of your attention, which has been his alone for all these years. This will depress him and possibly lead him to consider the

"Mellie"

Jean says, "Being a Basset, Mellie was stubborn and ignored much of what I said for most of her life. One of the phrases she knew and always responded to, however, was 'There are people outside.' When I said this, she always knew that she could run to the front window and bark her head off at someone walking down our street. One afternoon, I couldn't find Mellie anywhere. I looked all over the house and called her name repeatedly, then went in the backyard and looked and called for her. No response. Because she was old and feeble, I was beginning to panic. Then I finally realized what might work; I stood on the back porch and yelled, 'There are people outside!' Mellie came crawling out from under the back porch, walked right past me without a glance, and headed straight for the front window, looking for whoever needed to be barked at. From then on, I used 'There are people outside' as a test to see if I was being ignored or if my senior girl's hearing had indeed gotten worse."

new baby as a rival. To avoid this, make sure that he sees the arrival of the baby as a joyous event. This means that while the baby is present the dog gets special treats and belly rubs that he doesn't get at other times. This helps him see the baby as an ally and not an enemy. Please don't neglect your faithful old friend now. A friend of mine was gazing admiringly at his new baby when his old German Shorthair Pointer nervously nosed his hand. Larry looked down at his dog and whispered confidingly, "That's okay, Oscar. You're still my favorite." The dog was pleased and the baby didn't care.

How to Introduce a New Baby
Because you will know the baby is coming before she actually arrives, you can practice carrying a doll around and making sure that the dog finds it uninteresting. Some people play sounds of crying babies or bring home a blanket from the hospital that has the baby's smell on it. It also helps if your neighbor can keep the dog for a few hours until after the baby has arrived.

You will also have plenty of time to review basic obedience commands so that your senior will behave properly when asked to do so. You may want him to sit while you are changing the baby's diaper without his help investigating its contents.

With Children
While it's important for all children to learn to take care of the family dog, your senior should not be a living laboratory for child development. As the parent, you are the one responsible for feeding and caring for the dog, and although it's wonderful to teach your children how to do it, they need to be supervised. Even high school kids can "forget" to feed the dog and change his water. Their heads are filled with other things.

How to Keep Harmony in the Home
If you have adopted an older dog into your family, your children can learn to take care

of him. Older children can learn how to walk the dog and how to hold the leash properly. They need to learn to keep the dog off other people's property, and if old enough, how to pick up after him safely.

Children of any age can learn to check the dog's water bowl and help you feed him at breakfast or dinner. Older children can do this themselves but often need to be reminded to do it.

Young children need to be taught how to handle (or not handle) a dog. Proper petting techniques can be taught with a stuffed animal. All children need to learn that dogs must not be chased, yanked, hit, stepped on, yelled at, or poked. A child needs to learn that when the dog is lying in his bed, eating, sleeping, or walking away, he must be left alone. Also, children need to learn what and how many treats are safe for the dog and should not be allowed to hand them out unless supervised.

Some parents play a "doggy game" with their children in which the child pretends to be the dog and the parent plays the part of the child.

Young children need to learn how to behave appropriately around senior dogs.

They soon learn that it's not fun to be pinched or screamed at. Try explaining to the child that the dog is a "grandfather" or "grandmother" dog who may not want to play all the time but who enjoys quiet attention.

LIVING WITH SENIOR DISABILITIES

While a dog of any age can become disabled, senior dogs are most likely to be affected. Some common disabilities include back problems and paralysis, deafness, and blindness.

Back Problems and Paralysis

Partially paralyzed dogs can still enjoy a good quality of life, just as people in wheelchairs can. In some cases, the paralysis is permanent, but in others, the dog will recover some or all of his power of movement with some help from you.

Your first job—and the hardest—is to keep your dog clean. Many paralyzed dogs suffer from both urinary and fecal incontinence and have a limited ability to groom themselves. Unless you are scrupulous in this regard, your senior will feel bad, smell bad, and be more subject to disease and bladder infections. (Because of the neurological dysfunction that occurs with paralysis, the bladder may not empty fully, thus leaving the way open for infection. Ask your vet to perform periodic urine cultures to check for infection.)

Regular emptying of the bladder is one of the best ways to prevent bladder infections. In paralyzed dogs with spinal lesions above the level of the waist, you will probably have to manually express the bladder by pressing on it. (Your vet can show you how—it isn't difficult.)

You will need to bathe your dog at least every other day with a moisturizing shampoo to remove urine from his skin and fur. If the urine stays there, it can cause "urine scald" on his sensitive skin. For a quick cleanup, use a dry shampoo and baby wipes. You also can use "doggy diapers" that help to keep the house clean, although you must be vigilant about changing them.

In addition to bladder problems, your paralyzed pet may be subject to bedsores because he is not able to switch positions easily. The elbows, ankles, and hips are especially vulnerable. A machine-washable orthopedic bed, which is designed to protect pressure points, is absolutely essential.

You can purchase items to help a partially paralyzed or weak-limbed dog move more easily, such as special dog support slings and harnesses (for front or rear legs). These are designed to help your dysplastic, arthritic, postsurgical, or otherwise disabled dog move more comfortably and safely. Many paralyzed dogs who have good strength in the front legs benefit from a mobility cart. This is good for them both physically and psychologically. Other dogs may enjoy a trip in a pet stroller, in which they can enjoy

Recovering From Back Surgery

If your dog has had back surgery, physical therapy is one recovery strategy you might consider. There are actually certified canine rehabilitation practitioners, and if you can find one, you are in luck. The purpose of rehab is to build strength, and in the case of partially paralyzed animals, to increase their sense of "where their feet are." Three basic types of therapy are available: aquatic therapy, therapeutic exercise, and gait training. Most dogs require therapy daily for a few days, then two or three times a week for a month or so.

Mobility carts are available to help disabled dogs move more comfortably and safely.

fresh air and company from the safety of a wheeled conveyance. There are dozens of models to choose from—select one that is easy to assemble and has convenient dimensions and weight.

Deafness

Most older dogs experience some loss of hearing. However, the process is so slow that you may not realize it has happened, especially if you own one of those dogs who never paid any attention to you even when he could hear you. If your dog seems to be paying less attention to you and suddenly ignores the phone and doorbell, he may be losing his hearing. If you suspect that your dog has a hearing problem, take him to the vet to be sure. While most hearing loss is part of the natural process of aging, it also could be related to another problem, such as a tumor or infection in the ear.

You can usually get the attention of a deaf dog by stamping on the floor, clapping,

Dogs who are completely deaf can learn to respond to hand signals.

turning lights on and off, or using a laser pointer. Getting a whistle may help your dog hear you at a distance.

It is critically important to keep your dog on a leash at all times when he's not in the house or in the yard under your supervision, because even an elderly, supremely well-behaved dog may suddenly decide to run across the street after a squirrel. Attach a loud bell to his collar. If he gets away, he won't be able to hear you, but you may be able to hear his bell ringing.

When waking up a deaf dog, always touch him very gently on the shoulder. (That's the safest place.) If you have one of those dogs who "comes up swinging," use a long pole to wake him—no point in getting an accidental bite! You can gradually desensitize your dog to this startle reflex, to some degree at least, by touching his shoulder frequently and always giving a treat when you do so.

Dogs who have gone completely deaf can learn to respond to hand signals. In fact, if your dog is amenable to the idea, he can actually relearn commands in a simplified version of American Sign Language. You can make up your own signals, too, of course. The common sign for "good!" for example, is to smile and clap your hands together. Most dogs learn this one quickly, especially if there is a treat involved.

For support and information on deafness in dogs, visit the Deaf Dog Education Action Fund at www.deafdogs.org.

Blindness

Blindness, both partial and total, is a rather common affliction of older dogs. It can be caused by glaucoma, corneal problems, cancer, trauma, retinal diseases, or cataracts. Dogs who are losing their sight may become uncertain of their surroundings, especially at night; however, in most dogs, sight is lost so gradually that their owners are unaware of it, especially because their remarkable noses help them find their way.

Blind dogs require some extra care but can enjoy long and full lives. It is not the tragedy for them that it is for humans, and in fact, blindness seems to bother the dog owners more than it does the dog, who lives in a universe of rich smells and vibrant sounds. If you are patient with your blind dog, conservative about moving furniture around, and willing to make a few adjustments to his new lifestyle, there's no reason he can't go on happily for many years to come.

Don't baby your blind dog. He'll still enjoy walks and being outside in your company. Of course, you should never leave him alone outside or indoors in a strange place or with new furniture. Be consistent about his feeding and sleeping areas, and speak to him before touching him. Use a crate when he's by himself until he knows the house very well. Block his access to stairs. Talk to him, give him squeaky toys, and try in every way to enrich his world of sound and smell.

Give your senior time, and he will learn to navigate his way around. In fact, if the blindness has been coming on gradually, he may have already learned to do this so well that it comes as a surprise to discover he's blind! Make sure that you don't clip off his whiskers, which he can use to help guide himself around rooms. I know one dog who carried a stuffed toy in his mouth and used it as a "bumper." In fact, you can purchase a harness-like device that acts in much the same way, although most dogs seem preternaturally able to guide themselves.

You can help your dog by being super conscious of open doors, fireplaces, hot tubs, and sharp objects located at doggy eye level. Put a note on his collar that states he is blind, in the awful event that he becomes lost.

For support and more information on blind dogs, visit the Owners of Blind Dogs website at www.blinddogs.com.

Living with a senior dog is just that—living. It may be living at a slower and more relaxed pace than in the wild days of puppyhood, and that's mostly a good thing. Now that you are both older and wiser, you will have the time to smell, see, hear, or touch the remarkable wonders along the way. Don't be afraid to take it easy. Pleasures that are slowly savored last so much longer.

⊰ Senior Moment ⊱

Don't Worry

Don't worry—your blind senior will soon learn to navigate his way around the house.

Chapter 3

FEEDING YOUR SENIOR DOG

While diet is always a critical factor for an animal's health and well-being, it is especially critical in old age. Only in puppyhood does a good diet make more difference. Older dogs, whose systems are failing, need to get the best possible nutrition. This chapter will cover how to best feed your older dog, both in sickness and in health.

GOOD NUTRITION FOR A HEALTHY SENIOR

We are what we eat, and this is especially true for senior dogs. Because they have fewer "inner resources" to draw on and because they aren't as efficient at making some of their own vitamins as they used to be, their health depends on the nutrients they receive in the diet you feed.

Carbohydrates

Most dog food in the United States is full of carbohydrates—up to 40 percent in the case of some kibble. However, a carbohydrate-based diet is not natural for dogs and isn't healthy for them. Dogs are designed to be largely meat-eating animals, and while they will scarf up anything they can find for survival, as their ancestors did, they function best on the diet nature intended for them. This means that your dog's diet should be meat based, not corn or rice based; in fact, at least 75 percent of your dog's intake should be meat. Cut back on the carbs for your senior dog to make room for the extra protein and fat he needs without adding a lot of calories. What carbs you do add to the diet should be whole grains and vegetables, not sugar.

- **Function:** Carbs provide efficient, cheap energy and serve as building blocks for other biological components. They are also a heat source for the body when they are metabolized for energy. They can be stored as glycogen or converted to fat. Carbs also help to regulate protein and fat metabolism.

- **Sources:** Sugar, starches, and dietary fiber are all carbohydrates.

- **Senior Benefits:** The right carbohydrates are easily digested, which can be a plus for an older dog whose digestive system does not work as efficiently as it did when he was younger.

Special Carbohydrates: Dietary Fibers

Dietary fibers are indigestible carbohydrates.

- **Function:** Dietary fibers help to move food through the intestinal tract and

Fewer Calories, Higher Quality

In simplest terms, older dogs have less muscle mass than they used to, so they need fewer calories to maintain their bodies. At the same time, they need better nutrition as they age. For optimum health, feed fewer calories of a higher-quality food.

Carbohydrates provide your senior dog with energy

provide bulk, which causes an animal to feel full without adding extra calories.

- **Sources:** Fiber sources such as beet pulp, found in many commercial foods, help to maintain intestinal health for older dogs and enhances their ability to absorb age-essential nutrients. A diet containing fructooligosaccharides (FOS), a unique fiber source available in many senior commercial foods, maintains healthy intestinal bacterial populations to keep your dog's digestive system healthy.

- **Senior Benefits:** Older dogs are more prone to constipation, so many commercial senior diets are higher in fiber (3 to 5 percent) than regular adult food is. Wheat bran can be added to regular dog food to increase the amount of fiber.

If your old dog has a bout of diarrhea or constipation, try giving him 1 or 2 teaspoons (4.9 or 9.9 ml) of canned pumpkin (real canned pumpkin, not the sugary pie filling). It is loaded with fiber that helps stubborn bowels get moving but absorbs excess water from loose bowels. In other words, the same remedy helps both conditions! If the diarrhea or constipation continues, however, contact your vet.

Fats

Don't wince. Fat is not bad for dogs. Healthy dogs digest fats efficiently (90 to 95 percent) and so need a higher proportion in their diet than humans do to keep healthy.

- **Function:** Fats are an important energy source. Fat also makes food taste better (an important consideration in a senior dog's diet), which is why most dogs prefer any canned meat to dry kibble. Fats also deliver the fat-soluble vitamins A, D, E, and K and contribute to a healthy coat.

- **Sources:** Fats are primarily found in meats and vegetable oils.

- **Senior Benefits:** Fats are particularly important for dogs who have difficulty

The right amount of fats in the diet contributes to a healthy, shiny coat.

maintaining weight or who are picky eaters. On the other hand, fats also have twice the number of calories per gram as do proteins or carbohydrates, a factor you need to keep in mind when considering your older dog's slowing metabolism. Most commercial dry dog foods contain between 5 and 10 percent fat, sufficient for older, more sedentary dogs as far as energy needs go. However, most older dogs do much better on a diet of at least 14 percent fat. Too much fat, though, especially when given all at once, results in pancreatic problems. Insufficient fat makes for a dry coat and an inability to process fat-soluble vitamins.

Your senior dog's health depends on the nutrients he receives in his diet.

Omega-3 Fatty Acids

Fatty acids do all kinds of important things, including maintaining cell structure, aiding chemical reactions, and helping the skin remain supple, strong, and resistant to invaders. Omega-3s are essential fatty acids (EFAs), meaning that an animal needs them to live.

- **Function:** The role of omega-3 fatty acids is not really understood. It seems that sufficient amounts of omega-3s can lower blood pressure, reduce the clotting of blood platelets and therefore reduce blood clots, and reduce abnormal heartbeats.
- **Sources:** The best sources are marine fish oils, but flaxseed also has quite a bit. However, the body seems to be able to use the fish oil the most easily.
- **Senior Benefits:** Omega-3 fatty acids support joint health and help to keep the skin elastic, both important benefits for senior dogs. These fatty acids also may strengthen the immune system.

Omega-6 Fatty Acids

Omega-6s are other essential fatty acids.

- **Function:** Omega-6 fatty acids are critical to healthy skin and a healthy coat.
- **Sources:** Omega-6s are found in many plant products, such as sunflower seeds and oil and saffron oil. Poultry fat and pork fat have some too.

Nutrients at a Glance

Nutrient	Function	Sources	Senior Benefits
carbohydrates	regulate metabolism, provide energy	sugar, starches, dietary fiber	dietary fibers can relieve constipation
fats	provide energy, deliver fat-soluble vitamins	meats, vegetable oils	make food taste better, provide energy, help to maintain weight
proteins	maintain and heal; build muscles; build enzymes, hormones, hemoglobin, and antibodies	meat, fish, eggs, soybeans	maintain muscle protein stores
minerals	form bone and teeth, maintain fluid and acid/base balance, transport oxygen, aid in nerve and muscle function, produce hormones	various food sources	various functions—dogs require about 20 minerals in their diet altogether, some in very minute quantities
vitamins	aid in cellular metabolism	various food sources	enable cellular metabolic processes—required in minute amounts
water	plays an important function in every body process	fresh water crucial; water also can be found in canned foods and fruits like cantaloupe and watermelon	multitude of functions, including carrying other nutrients, flushing waste, aiding certain chemical reactions, helping to regulate body temperature, and providing shape and resilience to the body

- **Senior Benefits:** Senior dogs require gamma-linolenic acid (GLA). GLA is an omega-6 fatty acid that is normally produced in the dog's liver. In older dogs, GLA levels may be diminished because of changes in the enzyme responsible for production of GLA. By adding a natural source of GLA, like borage oil, skin and coat quality in senior dogs can be maintained.

> **Warning!**
> Dogs can overdose on fatty acids, so consult our veterinarian before supplementing them.

Fatty-Acid Warning

Know that dogs can "overdose" on fatty acids. If they are given too much or in an incorrect balance with other fatty acids, clotting problems and deficiencies of vitamin E can occur. If you are supplementing fatty acids yourself, talk with your vet about how to do so.

Cheaper dog foods may lack sufficient EFAs in the diet, resulting in a poor coat and dermatological problems. Your dog requires a complete and balanced diet with an adjusted ratio of omega-6 and omega-3 fatty acids to rejuvenate dry skin and help him develop a luxuriant, lustrous coat.

Proteins: Go Atkins!

A protein is a group of amino acids linked to each other in different quantities and sequences. About 50 percent of every cell in your dog's body is made of protein.

Dogs need more protein than people do. Although no optimum level has been established, even 30 percent of the total calories in their diet is not too much. (An exception is dogs with liver disease. Dogs with liver disease have a hard time removing ammonia, a waste product of protein, from the blood.)

If your dog doesn't get enough protein in his diet, he may show poor wound healing, dull coat, and muscular wasting. Excess protein is usually excreted from the body, except in cases where a dog has kidney or liver damage.

- **Function:** All animals need proteins for maintenance and healing. Proteins are critical for building enzymes, hormones, hemoglobin, and antibodies. They also build and maintain muscle, which is critical for seniors.

- **Sources:** Many foods contain proteins, including meat, fish, eggs, and soybeans. Dogs do best on meat- or fish-derived proteins; vegetable-derived proteins may be incomplete, meaning that they don't have enough of all the different kinds of amino acids your dog needs. They also can give your dog diarrhea. Dogs are carnivores by nature and need high-quality animal-based proteins to do their best. Ideally, a dog's diet should be about 75 percent meat and 25 percent vegetables.

Proteins are critical for building and maintaining muscle.

• **Senior Benefits:** Research has shown that senior dogs who eat a higher-protein diet maintain muscle protein stores better than those on a lower-protein diet. This research contradicts the conventional wisdom that senior dog foods should contain lower protein levels than adult maintenance formulas to avoid loss of kidney function. If your dog has significantly decreased kidney function, though, consult your vet. She probably will recommend a diet that is lower in protein—no more than 14 percent—which will ease the kidneys' workload.

Minerals

While the body needs a sufficient amount of minerals, the balance between them is also important because too much or too little of one mineral can adversely affect the functioning of the others. In a natural or good commercial diet, the minerals are balanced. This is why supplementation of only one mineral can be dangerous and should be done only under the supervision of your vet.

Typically, minerals are classed as macro- or micro-minerals, which simply means that the body needs a lot more of the former. Macro-minerals include calcium, phosphorus, magnesium, potassium, sodium, and chloride. The last three together are called "electrolytes." Micro-minerals include copper, iodine, iron, manganese, selenium, and zinc.

• **Function:** Minerals make up only about 7 percent of the body but are vital to its healthy function. They work with vitamins, enzymes, and even other minerals, helping to form bone, maintain fluid and acid/base balance, transport oxygen, make nerves and muscles function, and produce hormones.

• **Sources:** Various foods; different foods contain different minerals.

• **Senior Benefits:** Minerals maintain bone and muscle structure and regulate bodily functions, among other things. However, seniors may have more trouble absorbing minerals through the intestinal tract, which is why it may be wise in some cases but only under the direction of your vet, to supplement them. However, healthy dogs eating a quality diet generally receive all the minerals they need from their food.

Calcium

- **Function:** The body needs more calcium than it does any other mineral. Calcium is critical for bone formation, blood coagulation, muscle contraction, and nerve impulse transmission. Too little calcium in your senior's diet could lead to bone weakening as the body seeks to maintain its vital calcium levels. If the body has to steal from the bones to the get the calcium for other functions, it will.

- **Sources:** The main dietary sources for calcium are bones, dairy products, and legumes.

- **Senior Benefits:** Calcium keeps the bones strong and regulates heart function.

Copper

- **Function:** Copper is a critical element for many processes of the body, including the formation of collagen, bone and connective tissue, iron absorption, the development of red blood cells, and hair pigment. It also functions as an antioxidant. Most good commercial dog foods contain a copper supplement. Copper toxicity is rare. Older dogs have a harder time absorbing copper than younger ones, so the copper should be in a form other than copper oxide.

- **Sources:** Dietary sources of copper include liver, fish, grains, and legumes.

- **Senior Benefits:** Copper is an antioxidant, which helps to keep the cells healthy.

Iodine

- **Function:** Iodine is critical for the thyroid gland and the production of thyroid hormones. (Thyroid hormones regulate the rate of metabolism in the body.) Signs of thyroid deficiency include hair loss, weight gain, weakness, and irritability.

- **Sources:** Dietary sources of iodine include fish and iodized salt. (Commercial pet foods supplement iodine by adding potassium iodide, potassium iodate, sodium iodide, or calcium iodate.)

Phosphorous and calcium work together to keep your senior's bones and teeth strong.

- **Senior Benefits:** Because many senior dogs have a lower thyroid function, iodine is especially important for them.

Iron

- **Function:** Iron combines with copper and protein in the body to make hemoglobin, which carries oxygen in the blood. Iron is also an important component of the enzymes needed for energy utilization. A deficiency of iron causes anemia. Too much iron is extremely rare, but if this did occur, it could interfere with the absorption of phosphorus.

- **Sources:** Dietary sources of iron include liver, meat and fish, whole grains, and legumes. Commercial pet foods are well supplemented with iron. The iron should be in a form other than iron oxide or iron carbonate.

- **Senior Benefits:** Because iron is needed to make red blood cells, it helps to give older dogs needed energy. However, too much iron can be toxic. Never supplement this mineral unless directly advised by your veterinarian. This includes iron for anemic dogs, whose anemia may not be iron related.

Magnesium

- **Function:** Magnesium is needed for the absorption and function of several vitamins and minerals. It's also necessary for bone structure, enzyme functioning, and protein production.

- **Sources:** Dietary sources of magnesium include raw wheat germ, whole grains, soybeans, milk, bone meal, lamb meal, oat and wheat bran, beet pulp, and fish. Quality dog foods are supplemented with magnesium.

- **Senior Benefits:** A diet that is deficient in magnesium could result in weakened bone structure in older dogs. Dogs with heart failure may benefit from added magnesium. On the other hand, senior dogs at risk of oxalate bladder stones may benefit from a diet that is lower in magnesium. Consult your vet.

Manganese

- **Function:** Manganese is necessary for normal metabolic processes and enzyme functions in the body. It is found mainly in the liver but also can be found in the pancreas.

- **Sources:** Dietary sources include whole grains, nuts, eggs, and green vegetables. Dogs should receive 0.05 mg for every 1 pound (0.5 kg) of dog food they eat (dry matter basis). Most high-quality dog foods are well supplemented with manganese.

- **Senior Benefits:** A manganese supplement may help in the absorption of glucosamine, chondroitin, and other anti-arthritic supplements.

Calcium–Phosphorus Ratio

Older dogs have finished growing, so they require less calcium and phosphorus in their diets than when they were puppies. However, both are still an important part of the diet. Without the correct amount and percentage of phosphorus in the diet (1.2 parts of calcium for 1 part of phosphorus), calcium uptake is compromised. Older dogs need from 0.5 to 0.9 percent calcium and from 0.4 to 0.8 percent phosphorus in the diet daily on a dry matter basis.

Iron helps to give older dogs needed energy.

Phosphorus

- **Function:** Phosphorus is found in every cell of the body. It is necessary for utilizing calcium and so is critical for strong bones and teeth.
- **Sources:** Main dietary sources are meats, especially organ meats.
- **Senior Benefits:** Phosphorus, in combination with calcium, works to keep your senior's teeth and bones strong. Older dogs are actually more at risk from getting too much phosphorus than too little. Too much phosphorus may accelerate the rate of kidney disease, a common condition in older dogs.

Potassium

- **Function:** Potassium is found in high concentrations in the cells. It is necessary for the proper functioning of enzymes, muscles, and nerves. As an electrolyte, it is also necessary for maintaining the correct fluid balance in the body. Dog foods should contain at least 0.6 percent potassium (dry matter basis). Signs of potassium deficiency include cardiac arrest, appetite loss, and lethargy, although deficiency in general is quite rare.

- **Sources:** Potassium is plentiful in food, especially in fruits and vegetables. There is also a sufficient amount in meat. Potassium doesn't need to be supplemented unless the dog has chronic diarrhea, vomiting, or kidney disease, common conditions in older dogs.

- **Senior Benefits:** Potassium supplements may be helpful for older dogs with heart failure who are on potassium-leaching diuretics.

Selenium

- **Function:** In trace amounts, selenium works with vitamin E and certain enzymes to protect cells. Selenium deficiencies are rare in dogs, but signs include muscle weakness and heart problems. Signs of toxicity, a condition that occurs if the dietary intake goes above 0.9 mg of selenium for every 1 pound (0.5 kg) of food eaten (dry matter basis), include hair loss, lameness, anemia, and cirrhosis of the liver.

- **Sources:** Dietary sources of selenium include cereals and meats. Your dog needs 0.05 mg of selenium daily for every 1 pound (0.5 kg) of food he eats (dry matter basis).

- **Senior Benefits:** Selenium protects cells from oxidation, especially in combination with vitamin E. Many people feel that this reduces the risk of cancer in older dogs. Selenium also works with iodine to help thyroid function.

Commercial Vitamin Supplements for Seniors

Although most senior dogs get sufficient vitamins in their daily diet, several excellent commercial products, specifically designed for seniors, are on the market. These are important for dogs who are "off their feed" due to debility or sickness, but even generally, healthy older dogs can benefit from a multivitamin-mineral supplement. Choose one fortified with fatty acids, milk thistle for liver health, digestive enzymes, and antioxidants. Some also contain glucosamine/chondroitin to build cartilage and bromelain to ease joint discomfort.

Sodium and Chloride

- **Function:** Sodium and chloride are called electrolytes. Both sodium and chloride help to regulate the acid–base balance and maintain the balance of dissolved substances inside and outside the cells. Sodium is needed for the absorption of sugars and amino acids in the small intestine. Sodium, together with potassium, is also necessary for the transmission of nerve impulses. Chloride forms the hydrochloric acid in the stomach, which helps in the digestion of protein. A deficiency, although rare, causes excess urination, salt hunger, pica (desire to eat unusual substances), and weight loss. Obese dogs, hypertensive dogs, and dogs with kidney disease or certain endocrine conditions should avoid salt. Most commercial food is loaded with it.

- **Sources:** Sodium and chloride are found in salt, cereals, fish, eggs, dried whey, and poultry by-product meal.

- **Senior Benefits:** Senior dogs who are dehydrated may benefit from the supplementation of these important electrolytes.

Zinc

- **Function:** Zinc is important in the production of proteins and also improves a dog's coat. It is especially important for normal metabolism. Because zinc is not well absorbed by the body, it is often added to commercial diets as a supplement. Plants and fibers contain substances that bind zinc, so dogs fed a mostly vegetable diet may develop a zinc deficiency. Dogs with inflammatory bowel disease also may develop a zinc deficiency. A diet deficient in zinc will result in thin hair and crusty dermatitis. Oldsters with this problem may require a supplement. You can find a zinc supplement in good multivitamin supplements and in many fatty acid supplements.

- **Sources:** Meat and eggs are the most readily absorbed sources.

- **Senior Benefits:** Zinc helps to keep your older dog's immune system strong and helps him digest protein more efficiently.

Vitamins

A vitamin is an organic substance present in tiny amounts in food. You know them by their letters: A, B complex, C, D, E, and K.

- **Function:** Vitamins are essential to proper cellular metabolism. They work as essential enzymes, enzyme precursors, and coenzymes to aid metabolism. Vitamins A, D, E, and K are fat-soluble vitamins that are stored in fat-storage cells called lipocytes. Because these vitamins are stored in the body, oversupplementation can result in toxicity. Water-soluble vitamins, which include B complex and C, are excreted in the urine and so should be supplied every day.

- **Sources:** Vitamins are found in various foods.

- **Senior Benefits:** Aging dogs are often less able to make or absorb vitamins than younger ones are and may benefit from supplementation, which will improve their overall health. This is something to discuss with your vet.

Vitamin A

- **Function:** Vitamin A works to aid vision and maintain epithelial tissue, the tissue covering the internal and external surfaces of the body. An insufficient amount of vitamin A can produce night blindness and poor-quality skin and coat.

A deficiency of salt in the diet may result in pica, the desire to eat unusual substances.

- **Sources:** Dietary sources of vitamin A are liver, fish liver oil, yellow vegetables, and dairy products.

- **Senior Benefits:** Helps vision and maintains tissues and skin.

The B Vitamins

- **Function:** The B vitamins are essential for all dogs, including seniors, and some holistic vets recommend that B complex vitamins be supplemented for senior dogs. B vitamins include thiamin, riboflavin, pyridoxine, and biotin.

- **Sources:** Dietary sources of the B vitamins include meats, grains, and legumes.

- **Senior Benefits:** The B vitamins help to increase appetite, which is important for some old dogs who have a diminished appetite due to loss of smell or taste.

Fruits and vegetables are excellent sources of vitamins.

Vitamin C

- **Function:** The body uses vitamin C to make collagen, which forms connective tissue. Like most animals other than primates and guinea pigs, dogs can make their own vitamin C from glucose, but older dogs may benefit from supplementation. Consult your vet if you're thinking about supplementation.

- **Sources:** Dietary sources include fruits and vegetables.

- **Senior Benefits:** Because vitamin C has antihistamine properties, some theorists believe that it helps to protect against certain canine allergies. It may prevent the formation of some kinds of bladder stones. It may even fight cancer—both by preventing the occurrence of the disease and as a dietary supplement for cancer patients. Some studies seem to indicate that large doses of vitamin C result in lessened joint pain, although it can't treat the underlying condition itself.

Vitamin D

- **Function:** Vitamin D (the "sunshine vitamin") helps to regulate calcium and phosphorus in the blood and aids in nerve and muscle function. Too much vitamin D, a rare occurrence, could lead to calcium deposits in the heart, muscles, and other soft tissues. Deficiencies are historically more common than excesses.

- **Sources:** Sources of vitamin D include plain old sunshine, and to a lesser extent, dairy products and fish liver oil. The outer layers of the skin use ultraviolet radiation from the sun to convert vitamin D precursors into the real deal.

- **Senior Benefits:** Vitamin D helps to keep your aging dog's muscles strong. However, if he gets plenty of calcium and phosphorus in his diet, he is getting plenty of vitamin D.

Vitamin E (Tocopherols)

- **Function:** Vitamin E is important for the structure and function of cells and the metabolism of fats. It is an antioxidant that protects hormones from oxidation, which, as mentioned in Chapter 1, can damage good cells as well as bad ones. Many commercial foods add vitamin E as a preservative. Deficiencies of vitamin E cause cell damage and death in the muscles, eyes, heart, liver, and nerves.

- **Sources:** Dietary sources include cold pressed vegetable oils, wheat germ, meats, nuts, and green leafy vegetables.

- **Senior Benefits:** When used topically, vitamin E is an excellent wound healer and scar reducer. Some also consider this vitamin beneficial for arthritic dogs. It was once thought that vitamin E would help to prevent heart disease in older dogs, but this is no longer believed to be true.

Adding Antioxidants to the Diet

Antioxidants are naturally occurring nutrients. They help your older dog maintain health by neutralizing the peroxidation process of cellular molecules, a process that kills good as well as bad cells. Even though antioxidants occur normally in the body, it is important to add them to the diet in older dogs. Recent research has found that dogs fed a diet rich in antioxidants like vitamin E, lutein, and beta-carotene have better immune responses and vaccine recognition. (In other words, antioxidants allow vaccines to work better.) This is important for senior dogs, because as dogs age, immune responses can decrease.

Feeding Bones

Most of the nutritional benefits of bones are not in the bones themselves (which are mostly made of calcium phosphate) but in the meat, marrow, and cartilage that accompany them. Bones have no vitamins, no fatty acids, and only some practically indigestible protein in the form of collagen.

If you decide to feed bones to your senior dog, they must be both fresh and meaty for him to benefit. Your best choices are chicken legs and wings because these bones have a perfect calcium-phosphorus ratio. Beef and even turkey bones may be too hard.

Bones of any kind, but especially cooked bones, are dangerous for a dog's innards. They can splinter and perforate his intestine. In addition, bone chewing is the major cause of tooth breakage in dogs, especially in older animals whose teeth are not as tightly seated as when they were young.

Vitamin K

- **Function:** Vitamin K is essential for normal blood functions. Without vitamin K, blood cannot clot, and that's bad news if your dog gets a cut.

- **Sources:** Green leafy plants, liver, and some fish meals.

- **Senior Benefits:** Helps blood clot.

Water

Water is the elixir of life, so keep your older dog constantly supplied with clean, cool, accessible water. Normal dogs drink between 1 and 1.5 ounces (29.6 and 44.4 ml) of water per 1 pound (0.5 kg) of body weight per day. Of course, this varies with the temperature and the amount of water a dog gets in his food, with dogs who eat dry food needing to drink more water than dogs fed canned food. (Canned food can be 80 percent water; dry food is about 20 percent water.)

Some people don't provide their dog enough water when they leave home for the day because they feel that the dog will be less likely to urinate in the house. If this is your situation, please find another way to protect your home. The best way is to find a noontime dog walker or perhaps to install a doggy door. Restricting your dog to the kitchen is a better choice than depriving him of water. In fact, dogs who are given insufficient water are much more likely to develop bladder and kidney stones. Also, if your senior doesn't get enough water, he will become dehydrated, which can result in an electrolyte imbalance and thickened blood.

Some older arthritic dogs don't drink enough water because the pain of moving is greater than their thirst. In other cases, they won't drink stale, drooly water, even though they are very thirsty. Help your older dog get enough to drink by placing several bowls of cool water around the house so that he can get to them easily. And make sure that he gets enough bathroom breaks because older bladders aren't what they used to be.

- **Function:** Water carries other nutrients, flushes waste, aids certain chemical reactions, helps to regulate body temperature, and provides shape and resilience to the body. Owners should make sure that their senior dogs have easy access to fresh water at all times because it may be painful for arthritic dogs to walk long distances to get to their water bowl.

- **Sources:** Aside from the obvious, canned foods contain a certain amount of water, as do fresh fruits and vegetables.

- **Senior Benefits:** Seniors tend to "dry out" a little as they age, and so keeping them hydrated is of critical importance. Having plenty of water is crucial for all dogs but especially for those with diabetes or kidney disease, both common conditions in older dogs.

Keep your older dog constantly supplied with clean, cool, accessible water.

CHANGING TO A SENIOR DIET

As your dog ages, his dietary needs change. And just as senior dogs often need a different diet than their younger counterparts, they also may need a different diet from each other. One size does not fit all, and age is not the only criterion to consider. Your healthy senior dog may do best on a diet that is higher in fiber and lower in calories than a young adult's diet. A senior who is losing weight may need more calories. Dogs with significantly decreased kidney functions may need a diet lower in protein. Dogs with heart failure or bladder stones also may require a special diet. Your vet is the best person to help you make these determinations.

When to Transition to a Senior Diet

If you are feeding your dog a commercial diet, it is best to transition to a specially formulated senior diet at the appropriate age. While age is partly an individual process, it is partly dependent on size. Here is a general guideline. Always change your dog's food gradually (over the period of a week or two) to prevent diarrhea, which sometimes occurs with a complete and sudden changeover.

Weight Range	Age to Begin Transition
up to 20 pounds (9.1 kg)	7 years
21 to 50 pounds (9.5 to 22.7 kg)	7 years
51 to 90 pounds (23.1 kg to 40.8 kg)	6 years
more than 90 pounds (40.8 kg)	5 years

How to Transition to a Senior Diet

A diet transition is best done gradually over the course of a week or ten days to reduce the chances of gastrointestinal upset. Simply begin replacing a little of the usual food with the new food in increasing increments until the switch is complete. Keep in mind that this process will take longer if your dog is picky.

FEEDING SCHEDULES

Dinnertime is a dog's favorite 30 seconds—which is all it takes for some of them to gobble down their food. However, *when* those seconds take place can be an important decision.

Free Feeding

Free feeding is defined as allowing a dog to eat on his own schedule. While some people prefer to free feed their dogs, this is an idea that has no advantages except for making a dog owner's life easier. Dogs who are free fed tend to gorge themselves, which places them at risk for bloat—a disease with an incidence that increases with the age of a dog. It is also impossible to free feed if you have more than one dog, because one dog is likely to eat all the food.

Scheduled Feeding

Scheduled feeding means feeding a dog at a certain time every day. It gives a dog confidence to know that he will not be "forgotten" and allows his system to regulate itself—something that can be very important to a dog whose sphincter is not what it used to be. As a rule, it is best to feed your dog twice a day to reduce the chances of bloat.

CHOOSING THE RIGHT FOOD FOR YOUR SENIOR

Before choosing a food for your senior, make sure that he has a geriatric checkup. Certain conditions, such as bladder stones, diabetes, heart failure, liver disease, allergies, gastrointestinal problems, and canine cognitive dysfunction, respond favorably to a customized veterinary diet. These diets have been formulated to target and modify specific metabolic processes, including digestion, immune response, blood pressure, renal function, liver metabolism, and blood glucose levels. Veterinary prescription foods are offered for use only by or on the order of a licensed veterinarian and are prescribed for dogs with diagnosed disease conditions. Their purpose is not just nutritional; it's also therapeutic and so might be thought of as a "drug." Rely on the advice of your vet for the right prescription food.

If your dog is healthy, you have plenty of options. If you have decided to go the commercial diet route, choose a food that has been specifically designed for seniors. However, it's important to know that such descriptive words as "senior," "super-premium," "gourmet," and even "natural" have no standard definition or regulatory meaning. That's why you have to read the label.

The Importance of Dog Food Labels

Pet foods in the United States are regulated at the federal level by the FDA's Center for Veterinary Medicine (CVM). The CVM requires the following to be on the label:

Scheduled feeding involves feeding your dog at a certain time every day, which allows his system to regulate itself.

proper identification of product, net quantity statement, manufacturer's address, and proper listing of ingredients. Some states also have their own labeling regulations, adopting the model recommendations of the Association of American Feed Control Officials (AAFCO). These regulations address issues such as the product name, the guaranteed analysis, the nutritional adequacy statement, feeding directions, and calorie amount.

Foods for pet consumption do *not* require FDA approval before they are marketed, but they must be made with ingredients that are "generally recognized as safe" (GRAS) or that are approved food or color additives.

Guaranteed Analysis

The guaranteed analysis specifies the product's minimum percentages of crude protein and crude fat and the maximum amount of crude fiber and moisture.

Nutritional Adequacy Statement

The nutritional adequacy statement assures consumers that a product meets all of a pet's nutritional needs. This is guaranteed by the AAFCO and is arrived at through feeding trials (the preferred method) or by nutritional calculation and analysis.

Order of Ingredients

Pet food ingredients must be listed on the label in descending order by weight. However, the weight includes the moisture in the ingredient, and that can make it hard to know exactly how much "real" food they are talking about. For example, fresh meat is usually about 70 percent water, so it may be listed first—but there may be more grain (which tends to be drier) in the food than meat. In addition, different preparations of grains can be listed separately, so that if you added them up, there might be more grain than meat. This practice is called "splitting."

How to Pick the Best Food and Avoid the Worst

Because few people are investigative reporters, you must rely on the AAFCO's assurances that what you are buying is safe and nutritious. From there, the decision of what to feed is based on your personal preferences. If you're feeding a commercial diet, select a food that has a "life stage claim" recommending it for seniors. However, there is no "official" senior life stage that is recognized by the federal government. For the consumer, this means "buyer beware." However, large, well-established companies have an excellent record of producing good-quality food. Many of them do their own peer-reviewed research. Some smaller companies also produce excellent foods but can't afford the high rental rates to appear on grocery aisle shelves.

Different consumers have different "red flag" words that make them refuse to buy a product. For some, it's the word "by-product" (although some by-products have higher protein value than some muscle meats.) Some wish to avoid "beet pulp," while others look for it. For some people, artificial colors, preservatives, or flavoring are to be avoided. Others don't mind them. In general, a quality commercial food is AAFCO approved and has been tested by the company that manufactures it. That is your baseline.

⋘ Senior Moment ⋙

Mini Senior Special

If you have a small senior dog, select a specially formulated, energy-dense senior food with small kibble sizes to make it easier for your dog to eat.

If you decide to cook your own food for your dog, go about picking the ingredients the same way you would for yourself: Select fresh, high-quality meats and vegetables in season.

It is also an excellent idea to feed your dog a variety of foods. Not only do dogs dislike monotony as much as people do, but your chances of giving him complete nutrition increase when you serve a variety of foods. However, if your older dog absolutely refuses to change and doesn't seem to appreciate variety, don't force it on him.

When I shop for dog food for my three seniors (one of whom is well over 16 and still getting about), here's what I look for:

- foods that contain a specifically named meat source such as chicken (not just "meat meal")

- foods that contain probiotics (the addition of so-called "good bacteria" and yeasts) to help my elderly dogs digest their dinner more easily

- fruits and vegetables (other than corn) for their minerals, vitamins, and fiber

- foods that contain oats and barley for their many health benefits

- foods that contain sunflower oil for its high-quality omega-6 essential fatty acids

- foods that contain marine fish or flaxseed oil for its high-quality omega-3 acids

- foods that contain glucosamine/chondroitin with manganese to help the arthritic senior

Here's what I avoid:

- foods with artificial preservatives like BHA, BHT, and ethoxyquin

- foods with mill-run (grains that consists mostly of the hulls, not the "meaty" part of grain) or nonspecific grains

If you decide to feed a commercial food, choose one that is specifically formulated for seniors.

- foods with artificial dye or flavors
- foods with corn, wheat, beef, or soybean (many dogs are allergic to these ingredients)

TYPES OF DOG FOOD

Like human food, dog food comes in many varieties, including dry, semi-moist, canned, raw, and home cooked. What you select for your senior dog depends partly on his preferences, partly on what is convenient for you, and partly on what is best for him. And despite what some purists might say, it is not necessary to stick with one choice. It is perfectly permissible to switch from kibble or canned to home cooked or raw as your time and preferences indicate. In fact, I urge you to "experiment" a little to see how your dog responds. Just because he is getting on in years doesn't mean that he can't have interesting dining experiences.

Commercial Dog Foods

If you choose a commercial food, select one that is specifically tailored for older dogs. This means one that is higher in fiber with substantial, high-quality protein. Many senior foods are lower in fat and calories, but go the low-calorie route only if your dog is in fact obese. Because your dog's digestive system is not what it used to be, select a food that has a meat-based protein content rather than a plant-based one. Dogs were not designed to get their protein from plants, and older dogs especially have a hard time digesting them in large amounts.

While many commercial pet foods were barely adequate to sustain a dog in the past, the highly competitive dog food market is driving up the overall quality of commercial foods. Today, owners have more good choices than ever before; however, they also need to educate themselves to know what they're buying.

Your basic commercial choices are dry (kibble) and canned. A third option, semi-moist, usually contains too much sugar. There is no inherent difference in nutritional value between canned food and kibble, but almost all dogs prefer the former. Whatever your choice, select one that is designed for senior dogs.

Dry Food (Kibble)

Dry food is the top choice of most pet owners because it is inexpensive, stores well once opened, and doesn't smell. Kibble also has marginal value as far as scraping plaque from your dog's teeth when he chews. Dog with few or missing teeth, however, may have a difficult time with dry food. If your senior suddenly seems reluctant to eat his kibble, it's time to take him for a veterinary checkup.

Canned Food

Canned food has a higher water content and is more expensive than kibble, but many owners like to add it as topping for less palatable dry food and mix it in. Because it has a stronger smell than kibble, it's ideal for older dogs whose noses aren't what they used to be. Dogs with reduced smelling capacity often have a lower appetite as well (taste and smell are intimately connected) and so often appreciate canned foods. Canned foods have a long shelf life if they remain unopened. Once opened, though, they should be used in a day or so because they don't contain preservatives. The biggest disadvantage to canned food is that it is somewhat messy to handle. If your dog doesn't eat his canned food in 20 minutes, toss it out.

Semi-Moist Food

Semi-moist food is often attractively packaged, but it is really not a good choice for your

Seniors with few or missing teeth may have a difficult time with dry food.

senior dog. It is very high in sugar sucrose (up to 25 percent in some cases), which is used as a preservative. This does nothing but add empty calories to your dog's meals, something your senior certainly does not need. It's bad for his teeth, too, because the sugar promotes tooth decay.

Noncommercial Foods

Considering what the commercial pet food market is like, it's all right to feed your dog most food that is healthy for human beings. The old business about "Don't feed your dog table scraps" was a masterpiece of propaganda served up with relish by dog food manufacturers. Dogs thrive on fresh vegetables, chicken, beef, and fish. Many dogs also like fruits, including apple slices, melon, banana, and berries. (I once had a dog who carefully picked blackberries from our bushes.) Low-fat plain yogurt and small amounts of cottage cheese are also delightful treats. (Large amounts of dairy foods can be troublesome, however—most older dogs lack the necessary enzymes to process them, and diarrhea can result.)

In short, high-quality leftovers are good for your dog. Don't let anyone tell you otherwise. Avoid cramming your dog with junk food you shouldn't be eating yourself: cookies, potato chips, chocolate (which is toxic to dogs), hot dogs, and pickles. Many of these foods cause gastrointestinal upset, which can result in vomiting, diarrhea, and even pancreatitis. This is especially likely with high-fat foods to which your dog is probably not accustomed.

Home-Cooked Diet

A home-cooked diet is simply a diet that you prepare in your own home, just the way you do for yourself. Its only disadvantage is that it can be time-consuming to prepare. Owners who wish to attempt this should be sure that they are giving their dogs the proper nutrients in the correct ratio and should consult a professional before attempting it.

One of the most important factors to consider in a home-cooked diet is digestibility and "biological value"—in other words, how much of the proteins, fats, and carbohydrates are actually used by the dog. If you make your dog's food from human-grade ingredients, he's in luck, because foods offered for human digestion typically have a higher biological value than commercial pet foods. Because food is not cheap, it's nice to know that your dog is getting the most of out it.

One of the greatest advantages to a home-cooked diet is that you can tailor it exactly to your dog's needs—and you can keep it safe. Pet food recall scares remind us that

A balanced home-cooked diet is a healthy alternative for your senior dog.

commercial foods can be contaminated at any point: production, handling, processing, storage, or distribution. Commercial foods can be contaminated with *Salmonella*, *Staphylococcus*, and *E. coli*. And while the same contamination can affect human foods, in general, a closer eye is kept on these foods. Dogs are lucky because, as natural scavengers, they are pretty adept at handling bacteria, although of course outright poisonous chemicals can do them in. However, older dogs, who have less active immune systems, are more in danger of food contamination than younger ones are.

Cooking your dog's food improves its digestibility and kills disease-causing bacteria, and I strongly advise it for older dogs.

Raw Diet

One of the recent fads in dog feeding is the "raw diet," which is the feeding of uncooked foods, primarily meat, to a dog. Advocates believe that because this is the diet that most nearly replicates what a wolf eats, it is also best for a domestic dog. They point out that cooking food destroys some vitamins. However, raw foods are much less digestible than cooked foods, an important consideration for senior dogs, who often have problems digesting food anyway. And while dogs' ancestors may have spent their lives eating raw meat (as did our own before we discovered a good use for fire), modern dogs are not wolves. Elderly dogs have considerable trouble chewing and digesting a raw diet unless they have had experience with it. In addition, raw meat can be loaded with bacteria, including *Salmonella* and *E. coli*. People with immune deficiencies should not even handle raw meat.

Do your research and check with your vet or a qualified animal nutritionist before feeding a raw diet, especially if your dog has never been on a raw diet before.

Supplements

Healthy dogs of any age likely do not require any supplements to their diet. However, many people have experimented with adding herbs or other edibles to their dog's dinner. Most of this is harmless and may be helpful, but you should always consult with your vet before using any supplement.

While powerful scientific evidence is lacking, there is considerable anecdotal support for the benefits of certain herbs in the diet for seniors. Here are a few of them:

- **Alfalfa:** Is rich in vitamins and minerals, as well as eight amino acids, digestive enzymes, and even chlorophyll (for fresher breath). In addition, it may ease the pain of arthritis.

- **Beet root:** May reactivate cellular respiration rate and so "rejuvenate" tissues.

- **Cayenne fruit:** May help to stimulate aging bodily organs and has shown beneficial effects for diabetic dogs.

- **Chapparel herb:** May help to cleanse the lymphatic system.

Age-Defying Tip

Eating for Joint Health

It is well known that aging dogs have deteriorating joints, but some people are unaware that this process can be halted. Good nutritional management can maintain healthy joints and promote mobility. Consider supplementing your older dog's diet with glucosamine and chondroitin sulfate. These are naturally occurring compounds that help to lubricate joints, build strong cartilage, and break down destructive enzymes. They are safe and require no prescription, and you will be surprised to see how much difference it makes in your older dog's activity level. But be patient—because they build cartilage, which takes time, don't expect changes overnight.

Feed your senior treats in moderation—too many can make him gain weight.

- **Comfrey leaf:** Contains allantoin for cell proliferation and carries nutrients and minerals to glands. Also, it may be a digestive aid.
- **Kelp seaweed:** May stimulate the thyroid and is thus helpful for dogs with hypothyroidism.
- **Papaya fruit:** May be a digestive aid.
- **Parsley root:** A diuretic that may help heart patients.

Treats

Older dogs enjoy treats just as much as they did when they were puppies. If your dog is overweight, you can safely and inexpensively give him carrot slices as a treat—easy on the waistline and pocketbook—and they are good for him, too. Treats of any kind should be small enough for your dog to swallow easily, like a dice-sized cube of hard cheese.

Remember that treats contain calories, so these must be calculated into your dog's total diet. Commercial treats are often grain based, so be careful if your dog has an allergy to corn. Dogs do not need to be stuffed with treats—instead of throwing your oldster a treat every time he looks longingly at you, give him some loving attention.

If you are feeding commercial treats, research the manufacturing standards of the country of origin to make sure that the treats are AAFCO approved.

FEEDING FOR IMPROVED HEALTH

A good diet is the key to good health. Over the years, researchers have found that certain foods can help dogs recover from or manage diseases. Many of these foods, however, are prescription only and not suited to healthy dogs. Talk with your vet if you want to feed your dog to manage a particular illness or condition.

A prescription diet may be appropriate if your senior has a medical condition.

Moderate exercise will help to keep your senior at a healthy weight.

Feeding to Slow Canine Aging and Prevent Cognitive Disorder

Recent research has shown that a diet high in certain omega-3 fatty acids may play an important role in slowing brain aging. Currently, such foods are limited to prescription foods.

Feeding for Dogs With Struvite Stones

Older dogs can be prone to a buildup of crystals and stones in the urinary tract, which can cause painful and bloody urination and even blockage in your dog. One kind of stone, the struvite stone, can be managed with a prescription diet that has lower levels of magnesium and phosphorus. A prescription diet also will produce an acidic urine pH to help to dissolve struvite crystals.

Feeding for Dogs With Oxalate, Urate, or Cystine Stones

You can help to manage this condition (which must be treated first with surgery) and prevent recurrence of stones by selecting a diet with low mineral levels.

Feeding for Dogs With Heart Failure, Heartworm Disease, and Liver and Kidney Disease

Talk with your vet about a prescription food with lower sodium and increased omega-3 fatty acids. Such a diet helps to improve blood flow to the kidneys while reducing high blood pressure.

Feeding for Dogs With Gastrointestinal Problems

Several prescription diets are available for various gastrointestinal problems, including flatulence, diarrhea, and constipation, many with extra fiber or adjusted levels of other nutrients that can deal with these problems. These foods are by prescription only, because your veterinarian needs to know what is causing the symptoms before assigning the correct diet.

Feeding for Dogs With Food Allergies

Dogs with food allergies often benefit from a diet comprising novel proteins such as emu, fish, or duck. If you suspect that your dog has a food allergy, talk with your vet.

Feeding for Dogs With Arthritis

If your dog has arthritis, your veterinarian may recommend that you select a food containing adequate amounts of chondroitin, glucosamine, manganese, and omega-3 fatty acids to help keep your dog's joints limber. Although many nonprescription foods include these also, they may not be present in sufficient therapeutic amounts.

Food allergies can be managed by selecting a diet that does not contain the allergen.

Feeding for Dogs With Kidney Disease

Prescription diets are available to help dogs ease the load on their failing kidneys. Most of these diets are quite moderate in protein, but the protein that's in them is of the highest quality. High-quality protein (with the proper balance of amino acids) can be fed in lower amounts to get the same protein benefit. The best kidney diets are low in phosphorus and moderately high in animal-derived fat. Plant oils, especially the omega-6s, are not good for dogs with kidney disease. Talk with your vet for specifics. If your dog is not used to a higher-fat diet, he should be switched over gradually.

Feeding for Dogs With Liver Disease

The liver is a dog's largest internal organ and works to rid the body of toxins. Some prescription diets are available that have highly digestible high-quality protein to reduce the liver's workload and to help to regenerate liver tissue. Some diets add antioxidants.

Feeding for Dogs With Diabetes

Dogs with diabetes and other fiber-responsive diseases respond best to a commercial formula with lots of fiber. Overweight dogs and dogs with struvite stones also may respond well to a high-fiber diet.

SENIOR TALES

"Lizzie"

Diane relates, "The strangest food-related incident I have ever had with any dog was with a senior Beagle I had. Lizzie was terrified of her food dish. At first I thought it was the shininess of the metal, so I switched to a dull ceramic. She still would not approach the bowl. Plastic wouldn't work either. I tried playing hardball—not feeding her at all until she ate from a bowl. This "worked" but didn't alleviate her terror while she gobbled the food. I had about resigned myself to feeding her directly on the floor forever, when I tried paper bowls. For some reason known only in her deepest of hearts, this was acceptable, and she ate picnic style for the rest of her very long life. (She attained the age of 18.)"

FOOD-RELATED PROBLEMS

While no one can live without food, the wrong kind or the wrong amount can lead to problems.

Health Issues

Most health problems relating to food are actually caused by your dog eating too much—or at least too much of the wrong thing. Some of the most common health issues include food allergies and flatulence.

Flatulence

Dogs who are regularly flatulent may be eating a food that is too high in corn or other carbs. Try changing his diet to one without corn or beans.

Food Allergies

Food allergies are not very common in dogs; in fact, it's estimated that they account for only 10 percent of allergic reactions. Still, they can occur—and old age is not a protection. A dog can develop an allergy at any age, even to a food he has been eating for years. Here is a list of the foods that most commonly produce allergies in dogs (in order of frequency):

- horse meat
- beef
- pork
- lamb
- poultry
- dairy products
- eggs
- fish
- corn
- soy
- preservatives and dye
- rawhide chews

Keep in mind that even premium foods can cause food allergies. It's the ingredient itself that triggers the allergy, not the quality of the ingredient. Food allergies cannot be cured, but they can be managed by selecting a diet that does not contain the allergen. Your veterinarian will help you select a specific diet for your dog, although it might take some experimentation.

Toxic Foods

While no one would purposely feed their dog something poisonous, it's important to remember that many common human foods are in fact very dangerous to dogs. Here are a few of them.

Potbelly

A dog with a potbelly may be more than just fat. He might have abdominal fluid, an enlarged spleen, Cushing's disease, or a tumor. Don't ignore it.

Alcohol

Keep alcoholic drinks out of reach of your dog. One ounce (29.6 ml) of a 20- to 40-proof alcoholic beverage can put a small dog in a coma.

Chocolate

Most dog owners know that chocolate is bad for dogs—but how bad depends on the individual dog, the amount, and the kind of chocolate devoured. Chocolate contains a chemical called theobromine that is toxic to dogs in varying degrees. Some dogs seem to be able to eat a fairly large amount of chocolate with no dire effects. Others might suffer from a much smaller amount.

Signs of chocolate poisoning in dogs include hyperactivity, vomiting, diarrhea, excess urination, nausea, seizures, irregular heartbeat, and coma. Signs usually begin within a few hours of ingestion but can take up to 36 hours to appear. If your dog has gobbled up the chocolate, take him to an animal hospital or veterinarian immediately. The best results follow early diagnosis.

Cocoa beans, cocoa powder, baking chocolate, and dark chocolate are the worst. Milk chocolate, chocolate drink mixes, and white chocolate are less dangerous.

Grapes and Raisins

In the past few years, it's been noted that ingesting large amounts (more than 9 ounces [266.2 ml]) of grapes or raisins can be toxic to dogs, causing kidney failure. The precise toxic substance responsible has not yet been determined.

Macadamia Nuts

These can cause a temporary rare leg weakness or paralysis in dogs.

Onions

As little as 1/4 cup (59.1 ml) of onions can cause hemolytic anemia in dogs.

Table Scraps

While some well-chosen leftovers provide a delicious and nutritious addition to your dog's diet, ill-chosen scraps piled on your dog's plate can result in misery for both of you. Dogs who are not used to a high-fat diet are especially in danger of developing pancreatitis from those fatty scraps. Most older dogs also don't have the enzymes to digest dairy products. I am not saying that all human food is bad for dogs—quite the contrary—but you need to be aware of what you are feeding your dog. He is not a garbage disposal.

⋘ Senior Moment ⋙

Nondietary Cause of Obesity

In older dogs, a significant nondietary cause of obesity is an inadequately functioning thyroid gland, which slows the rate at which dogs metabolize their food.

Obesity is common in older dogs because they have a slower metabolism and decreased activity level.

Xylitol

This is an artificial sweetener found in some gums and candy. Dogs who eat large amounts of it can suffer a dangerous drop in blood sugar that can last for hours. Never feed your dog anything sweetened with this.

Weighty Issues

Senior dogs run the gamut from being severely underweight to being grossly overweight. In most cases, generally healthy older dogs tend to be overweight, especially because their humans like to feed them. Other older dogs may lose weight, particularly if they are suffering from an illness, like cancer. Both conditions can be dangerous.

Obesity

One quarter of all dogs in the United States are overweight, a condition that has become epidemic in the canine world. It is especially common in older dogs. These animals tend to gain weight because they have a slower metabolism and decreased activity levels.

And while obesity is dangerous to a dog of any age, it is particularly damaging to older dogs' joints and heart. Obesity can complicate or even cause many other conditions, too, such as arthritis, liver disease, diabetes mellitus, cancer, cataracts, hypothyroidism, incontinence, and respiratory problems.

While some breeds, like Salukis, tend to be thin, and others, like Bulldogs, tend to be more portly, you should always be able to feel (if not see) the ribs on your dog. If you can't, or if he does not exhibit a narrowing at the waist when looked at from above, he is probably overweight. Your vet, by the way, will be happy to give you her opinion if asked.

One way to go about getting your senior to lose weight is to cut down on his calories by simply reducing the amount he eats. In some ways, this is preferable because it doesn't force your old dog to change from eating the foods he loves. It just means feeding him less of them.

Some recent research in dogs also indicates that L-carnitine, which is a vitamin-like compound made in the body from amino acids, helps to reduce weight in obese dogs by escorting fat into cellular mitochondria, which is then turned into energy. Consider such as a supplement for your obese dog.

Another way to help your dog lose weight is to put him on a special weight-reduction diet. These special diets are usually low-fat, high-fiber diets that seem to promote weight loss better than simply feeding smaller amounts of a high-fat diet. (Fat contains about twice as many calories as proteins or carbohydrates.) The fiber also seems to help dogs feel "full." In addition, unless your regular dog food provides more than enough vitamins and minerals, by feeding less of it, you may be depriving your dog of needed nutrients. So if you simply feed less of his regular diet, you may have to add supplements.

One caution, though. The directions, even on a diet food, may instruct you to give enough food to maintain your dog's present weight. (It's a legal thing—otherwise, the food can't be advertised as being sufficient to keep the dog alive by regular feeding.) Diet foods should have another panel that tells you how much to feed to help your dog *lose* weight—those are the directions you need to follow. There are many excellent prescription weight-loss diets on the market, and there are also some nonprescription brands that are formulated for this purpose.

Good diet foods usually have a fat content of 5 to 12 percent (dry matter basis) and increased fiber (7 to 30 percent). Fiber has several healthful effects for weight loss: It stimulates chewing, slows the movement of food from the stomach (making the dog feel full), and stabilizes the blood glucose level (to reduce that hungry feeling). However, be aware that a very high amount of fiber leads to flatulence and increased stool volume. You

Dogs are carnivores who need high-quality animal-based proteins to do their best.

Moderate exercise, like swimming, will help your senior lose weight.

don't want to skimp feeding protein, either, even in a reducing diet. The food should have at least 25 percent protein and an adequate level of vitamins, minerals, and fatty acids in the form of fish oils.

To make the weight-loss process easier on your dog, feed him two or even three small meals each day rather than one large meal. This might reduce begging as well. Or you can measure out the food allotment for the day, then give half for breakfast with the rest doled out throughout the day in place of treats. But to do this right, you need to accurately measure the amount.

Don't forget the exercise component! Moderate exercise is safe, is healthy, and will contribute measurably to your dog's happiness. If you have an opportunity for your older dog to swim, for example, so much the better.

The Underweight Senior

As dogs advance into the golden years, many begin to lose weight. This is not, as many people believe, "normal." Older dogs may lose muscle mass, but their weight should remain in the same vicinity as previously.

Obesity and Genetics

Not all dogs are fat because they are piggish eaters. Genetic predisposition and hormonal problems such as low thyroid levels also can be at fault.

Consult your veterinarian to determine if there is a physical cause for unexplained weight loss. Many illnesses, such as cancer, diabetes, kidney problems, and pancreatic ailments, can have this effect. Dogs who have suffered a traumatic injury are also prone to weight loss because they dedicate most calories to healing the wound. In addition, dental problems may make eating so painful for an older dog that he stops eating just to avoid the pain.

If there is no underlying medical cause for your dog's thinness, he just needs to consume more calories in an easily digestible form. Aim for gradual weight gain, adding about one and a half times the amount of food he has been getting previously. Don't let your older dog gorge on food, though. This puts him at a risk of bloat and other problems and means that he has less chance of maintaining his new weight. If your dog has been eating only once a day, increase it to twice.

If your dog is not sick in general, he may just be sick of his diet. Dogs on a kibble diet, for instance, often have a hard time chewing it as they age, and sometimes switching to canned food will do the trick. You also can try adding broth or gravy to your senior's kibble to soften it and give it some flavor, or warm the food to about 100°F (37.8°C) to make it more aromatic. Consider adding a little grated cheese or yogurt to make his food taste better.

Your dog is what he eats, and what he eats is mostly up to you. After all, he can't open the refrigerator himself and cut up some carrots for a snack. By putting good, healthy food in his dinner bowl, you'll be doing your bit to keep him around a long, long time.

Chapter 4

GROOMING YOUR SENIOR DOG

Older dogs seem to care less about their looks than do younger dogs. They are less likely to groom themselves, and their lower level of exercise means that they are less likely to keep their nails trimmed naturally. Luckily, your older dog has you to pick up the slack.

Besides, there's a positive side to all this—an older, wiser dog is much less likely to engage in foolhardy enterprises like skunk chasing and sap rolling, grooming jobs that no one wants.

COAT AND SKIN CARE

Good grooming starts from the inside with complete nutrition that supplies proper protein and essential fatty acids to make your dog's coat shine. Smart dog owners know that regular brushing and bathing not only keeps their older dogs looking great but even improves their health.

Brushing

Senior dogs often have drier skin than their younger counterparts. This condition can be improved by frequent brushing that gets the circulation going and the natural oils transported around the skin.

A short haircut may be more comfortable for your senior dog.

Choosing the correct brushing tools for your dog depends on his coat type. What is appropriate for a Komondor is not suitable for a Greyhound. I generally use combs to remove mats and tangles, and brushes to get rid of dead hair, surface dirt, and dander. Always comb and brush your dog *before* bathing. If your poor old dog is already matted to the skin, you may have to have him shaved by a professional groomer and start over.

Supplies

Here are some of the most common brushing tools and what they are used for:

Brush your senior gently, being careful not to scrape his delicate skin.

- **Flea comb:** This fine-toothed comb has more uses than just checking for fleas. If you have a short-haired breed, it helps to remove the shedding undercoat quickly and easily.

Grooming Supplies

- brushes
- combs
- doggy toothbrush and toothpaste
- ear cleanser
- eye wash
- hair mat removers
- nail clippers
- pet clippers
- shampoo and conditioner
- shedding rake
- styptic powder

- **Greyhound comb:** A double-sided steel comb that has wide teeth on one end and narrow teeth on the other. Despite the name, a greyhound comb is useful for dogs with long coats. After brushing, use the wide end first to remove the bigger tangles, then the small end. The pointed tip can be used to "de-mat" the hair. You also can use it to fluff a coat during drying.

Hand Stripping the Coat

Terriers often have their coats hand stripped if they are being shown. This is a time- and labor-intensive procedure that a senior dog does not need. Simply have his coat clipped. This may result in a coat that is not completely "correct" as far as texture goes, but your senior won't mind a bit.

- **Rake:** This wide-toothed implement is excellent at removing the shedding undercoat without damaging the outercoat.

- **Rubber curry comb, grooming mitt, or hound glove:** The nubby implements speed up the shedding process and help short-coated dogs shine.

- **Slicker brush:** A wire-bristled brush embedded in a rubber backing. These are available in different sizes and are useful for all types of coats, especially when you want to remove loose hair. In some cases, the bristles are straight, but if your dog has a long, thick coat, you'll be better off with the curved-bristle type. Always groom down to the skin without actually scraping the skin—that's called "slicker burn."

- **Stripping knife:** This implement is used on harsh-coated dogs like terriers. It removes hair but keeps the desired texture of the coat.

- **Thinning scissors:** If you own a long-haired breed, thinning scissors help to remove some of the "bulk" of the coat, making it less likely to mat.

How to Brush Your Senior

Apply the brush in long strokes along the body. Begin at the head and proceed toward the rear. Do ticklish sections like the sides, ear silk (on some dogs), and belly last. Don't forget to trim or clip hair between the paw pads and under the tail.

Don't press too hard when brushing or you could cause a "burn" to your older dog's more sensitive and fragile skin. If you encounter a mat, use a mat breaker or insert the end of the comb to try to loosen it. If this doesn't work, simply cut the mat out. Resolve to brush your dog more frequently next time so that no mats will form.

If you have a short-haired dog, follow up with a hound glove to improve the shine of the coat.

Bathing

Old dogs often acquire a certain "old dog smell" that is unpleasant to most of us. A quick bath will get rid of it. Frequent bathing with gentle shampoo will not destroy your dog's coat. Instead, it will loosen dead hair, remove odors (and any critters that may have temporarily lodged there), and make him feel clean.

When bathing your senior, first wet him down to the skin with lukewarm water.

Supplies

- **Bathtub-restraining device:** Consider a bathtub-restraining device, a noose-like attachment that keeps the dog in the tub. However, never leave a restrained dog alone in the bathtub.

- **Cotton balls:** For keeping shampoo and water from entering the ears.

- **Eye ointment:** For protecting the eyes from shampoo and water.

- **Nonskid rubber mat:** Older dogs can be a little shaky on their feet, so the nonskid mat makes a bath a much more pleasant experience. It also protects your bathtub from being scratched.

- **Shampoo and conditioner:** Just as for people, there's a canine shampoo for every type of hair. Some kinds are designed especially for white dogs, black dogs, or coats of specific textures, like Poodle or terrier coats. If you add a conditioner, your senior's skin will remain soft and pliable.

- **Scissors:** Have small, sharp scissors on hand in case you encounter a mat while bathing your dog.

How to Bathe Your Senior

Bathing a dog is not very tricky, although it is important to wet him right down to the skin with lukewarm water. (Be careful about the water temperature—older dogs do not enjoy being scalded or frozen and are much more sensitive to temperature extremes than they used to be.) Then, lather him all over with a mild shampoo. Be gentle. Speak calmly or even sing to your old dog while you're bathing him. He won't care if you're

Removing Dog Hair

Where there are dogs, there is hair. Removing dog hair is one of the special thrills of dog ownership. You'll be happy to know that regular grooming and bathing reduces the amount of dog hair floating around the house. Most of what's left over can be vacuumed up, but stubborn hair needs the assistance of a lint roller. If you have misplaced the lint roller, masking tape works just fine. Roll it around your hand with the sticky side out. It will be full of hair before you know it! You also can use lint rollers directly on your dog.

off-key; your pleasant voice will calm him. If your dog has seasonal allergies, bathe him regularly with a hypoallergenic shampoo in summer to remove allergens that adhere to the skin. If you need to use a medicated shampoo for his skin, make sure that it stays on the dog for the allotted length of time.

For the face, use a warm, damp washcloth and be careful not to let water get in the ears or eyes. If soap residue is left in the hair, it can irritate your dog's skin. It will probably take twice as long to rinse the dog as it did to wash him. Rinse well!

Finally, towel-dry him thoroughly, and don't forget to use plenty of towels. You can buy chamois-type towels that really soak up the moisture. If your dog's coat is very thick, use a handheld hair dryer on low or medium to dry him. However, unless your dog is used to a hair dryer, I would recommend just using towels. Seniors often don't appreciate the noise and commotion of the dryer.

Because the coats of older dogs tend to be dry, more frequent brushing and a special shampoo and conditioner may be called for. Adding conditioner to the dog's coat and then brushing the dog with the conditioner still in will help to release shedding hair. Then rinse the conditioner out and towel-dry. For the utmost chic, you may want to add a finishing spray. Apply while the coat is still wet. These sprays seal the coat with silicone to make it lie flat. The coat will shine and resist matting. Use sparingly, though, or the coat can acquire a rather plastic feel.

EAR CARE

One easy way to check your oldster's ear health is to smell his ears. Start by smelling them when you know they are clean and healthy to establish your baseline. Keep in mind that foul or yeasty smells signal an infection, as does redness or irritation. While deafness is more common in older dogs, sometimes what appears to be deafness is simply a buildup of wax in the ears. (For information on ear-related problems in senior dogs, see Chapter 8.)

Supplies

- **Cotton balls:** Use cotton balls (not swabs) to remove wax and dirt.
- **Ear cleaner:** Get a good, nonalcohol-based commercial ear cleaner.
- **Paper towels:** For drying the ears.

How to Clean the Ears

Begin by cleaning the earlobe, removing dirt, wax, and debris. Then, proceed to the cartilage. The ear canal is shaped like an "L," so you will not be able to manually clean the entire ear; it's safest to just to clean the parts you can see. Use a paper towel when you're finished to dry the ears.

EYE CARE

Improper eye care can lead to infection—just what your older dog does not need. If you have a breed that normally has a lot of hair around the eyes, it will help to trim it away with blunt-tipped scissors. This will keep dirt, irritation, and infection to a minimum.

A healthy dog's eyes should be wide open, with a clear center and pupils that are the same size. (If they are of unequal size, a neurological problem could be present.) The whites of the eyes should be pure white with no redness. Older dogs may have a greenish tinge to their eyes, but this is a normal characteristic of aging and nothing to worry about. The tissue beneath the lower lids should be a healthy pink.

SENIOR TALES

"Dusty"

While it is well known that most dogs dislike having their ears cleaned, there are some who are smart enough to understand its benefits. My friend Frieda Rose had a senior pointer named Dusty who had once suffered a bad ear infection. Somehow he figured out that the ear cleaning had a magical effect on his ears. Ever after, Frieda Rose would call out, "Dusty! Time for the cotton balls!" and he would shiver in delight and actually *run* to the bathroom in joyful anticipation. His delight did not extend to baths or nail clipping, unfortunately, but that old dog had the cleanest ears in town.

Supplies

- **Eye wash:** Use regular eye wash to clean an uninfected eye.
- **Soft cloth, presoaked eyewash cloth, or cotton ball:** Use to clean your dog's eye area daily.

How to Clean the Eye Area

Clean your senior's eye area daily with a cotton ball or soft cloth. You can use regular eye wash (sterile buffered saline) to clean the eye; however, this will not be helpful if the eyes are red or infected. (In that case, check with your vet right away.)

If there is no redness or irritation but just "gunk" in the corners of the eyes, simply wipe the corners with a soft, damp cloth or cotton ball. If the "gunk" keeps recurring, it could be a sign of dry eye, so talk with your vet.

NAIL CARE

If you can hear your dog's nails clicking on the floor, you know it's that time again. Untrimmed nails can break off, which is not only painful but very bloody. The frequency with which your dog's nails must be clipped depends on how much exercise he gets on hard surfaces like pavement.

You should be an old pro at nail clipping by this time, but if you've always been too nervous to try it, or if you have adopted an older dog with horrendous nails, I can assure you that it's not really difficult.

Supplies

- **Cornstarch or styptic powder:** This will stop the bleeding if you accidentally nick the quick.
- **Nail trimmer:** Purchase a nail trimmer designed specifically for dogs. You can buy one from your veterinarian or at a pet supply store. Select a pair that is comfortable in your hand, easy to clean, and appropriate for the size of your dog. Some people prefer guillotine-style clippers, especially for small dogs. It's easy to slide the nail through the opening and clip the nail. The main problem with this kind of clipper is that it doesn't work so well with bigger dogs. The edges also seem to dull quickly. I prefer the scissors-type clippers, which have semi-circular blades that stay sharp longer and can be used on thicker-nailed or bigger dogs.

Nail Health

Crooked, dry, or cracked nails may be a sign of a fungal infection or a poor diet.

If your senior is not used to having his nails trimmed, start slowly.

How to Trim Your Senior's Nails

First, learn his nail anatomy. The most important thing to know is that inside the center of each toenail is the "quick," the blood and nerve supply for the nail. This is what you want to avoid cutting. It is easily seen as a pinkish line in white nails but invisible in black ones. These nails require a little guesswork. The best way to do dark nails is to clip a tiny bit off the end and then look. If the area is "dead," you will see a gray or white spot in the center and can clip further. If the area is dark, you will know that that is where the quick begins.

If your dog is not used to having his nails trimmed, start slowly. A few dogs will sit on your lap or lie quietly on a table, but others must be restrained. Some dogs respond better if they are sitting on the floor, and some will allow a groomer or vet to do the job but not the owner.

Cut the nail quickly and firmly. Don't be squeamish! The general rule is that the

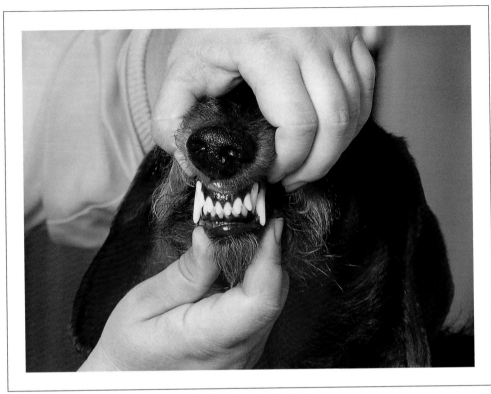

Visually inspect your dog's mouth for cracked, chipped, or missing teeth.

nail, which usually curls downward, should be even with the paw pad. Clip whatever hangs over. Always clip the nail from underneath, not from the top. Clip at a 45-degree angle.

After you clip the nail, you may want to file it smooth. If you cut too much by mistake, use some cornstarch or styptic powder to staunch the bleeding. The bleeding should stop within about five minutes. If it doesn't, call your vet.

DENTAL CARE

Your older dog needs his teeth brushed every day, just as you do. Good dental care keeps his breath fresh, his teeth brilliant, and his gums healthy. The older your dog is, the more he needs you to help him care for his teeth.

Supplies

- **Doggy toothbrush:** Special canine toothbrushes are available that have two heads of different sizes that are conveniently angled for a dog's teeth. You also can use a rubber finger cap with bristles or even a soft, damp cloth wrapped around your finger if your dog objects to a toothbrush.

- **Doggy toothpaste:** Dog toothpaste can be swallowed safely and comes in dog-friendly flavors, such as liver and chicken. Never give your dog human toothpaste.

How to Care for the Teeth

First, check the oral cavity for cracked, chipped, or missing teeth; off-color gums; strange odors; or anything else that doesn't look right. The great thing about this is that dogs who are used to having their mouths checked are less troublesome when it comes time to take a pill or when they have to have their mouths inspected by a veterinarian.

If your dog hasn't had his teeth cleaned in a long time or if they are dirty, you need to have them professionally cleaned. Brushing isn't very useful if your dog's teeth and gums are already in bad shape.

Try to brush your dog's teeth after every meal. If this isn't realistic for you, do it as often as you can. You may have to start slowly. Dogs not used to having their teeth brushed may object to the process and resist. As you brush, concentrate on the outside surface of the teeth. It's not only the easiest, but it's also the place where the plaque tends to form.

To complement your newfound great brushing techniques, make sure that your older dog gets a complete professional dental checkup every six months. During the exam, the vet will make a visual and manual inspection of the teeth, looking for gum disease, discoloration, loose teeth, tongue condition, and indication of pain. Some dogs will need a short-acting anesthesia to have the job done properly. (Many dogs just aren't that cooperative about dental exams.) An X-ray may be done to detect hidden periodontal problems and tooth abscesses that would otherwise be missed.

ANAL SAC CARE

The anal sacs are two small glands just inside your pet's anus, packed with terrible-smelling but completely normal secretions. Their purpose is not entirely understood. Wild animals can empty them at will to mark territory or for self-defense, but domestic dogs can't seem to do this. The sacs do usually empty when a dog defecates, but sometimes they become impacted, and you'll see the

◄ **Senior Moment** ►

Tooth Loss

Many older dogs experience tooth loss leading to problems in chewing, which can in turn lead to appetite and behavioral changes.

If your senior has a difficult coat to care for, consider hiring a groomer.

dog scoot around on his rear end. Older dogs may have more trouble with their anal sacs than younger ones do.

How to Empty the Anal Sacs

You can learn to empty the sacs by holding a tissue against the anus on each side and squeezing the sac gently. (Ask your vet for a demonstration.) Sometimes it takes several tries. However, if an impacted anal sac is not emptied, it can form an abscess and rupture out through the skin. This situation calls for veterinary treatment and a course of antibiotics.

If your dog continues to have trouble with his anal sacs, you can try switching him to a higher-fiber diet. This produces a bulkier stool that may help to empty the anal sacs when the dog defecates. In severe cases, you can opt for an anal sacculectomy, a surgical procedure that permanently removes the sacs.

FINDING A PROFESSIONAL GROOMER

If you don't have the time or energy to groom your dog, especially one with a difficult coat, think about hiring a groomer. Don't just run to the telephone book, though—ask around. Your vet probably knows some good ones, as do your dog-owning friends or neighbors. Take a look at the best-groomed dogs in your neighborhood, and ask the owners who their groomer is.

Before you commit your pooch irrevocably, stop by the prospective grooming shop and talk to the groomers. A brief chat should reassure you. If the place doesn't look clean, or if you don't like the way the employees are handling the dogs, find a better shop. Whomever you select should understand the special needs of older dogs. Most good groomers do.

Expect to answer some questions yourself—about how you want your pet groomed and any special care your pet may need during the process. In most cases, you'll be seeking an easy-care "'do" that will flatter your dog without making him look silly.

Good groomers require that you have proof of vaccinations for your pet. This makes perfect sense. No groomer wants a client showing up with a dog sneezing from kennel cough! You also should walk your dog before arriving so that he won't be uncomfortable waiting to "use the facilities" while lining up for his haircut. And make sure that your dog is reasonably well behaved. A groomer is a groomer—not a dog wrangler or trainer.

A well-groomed senior is not just a credit to his owner—he is a healthier, happier pet who is so pleasant to be around that you'll be begging *him* to come up on the couch to snuggle with you.

Age-Defying Tip

Hair Clipping for Better Health

Older dogs, especially those belonging to one of the hairier breeds, frequently benefit from some extra clipping around the anal area. The last thing he or you need is fecal matter becoming stuck under there. This seems to be a problem with older dogs whose bowel movements are not as well formed as those of younger dogs. Clipping now avoids a big mess later and will reduce the chances of infection. Clipping the anal area is as much a health enhancer as it is a cosmetic benefit.

≪ *Chapter 5* ≫

TRAINING AND BEHAVIOR

"Old dogs can't learn new tricks." This is probably one of the least accurate proverbs in existence. As human beings continue to learn all their lives, so do dogs. They can learn basic commands, they can learn to behave, and they can even learn tricks.

UNDERSTANDING YOUR SENIOR DOG

Dogs have different personalities, partly depending on their individual souls, partly on their breed or type, and partly on their experience with human beings. Some dogs are basically loyal and submissive, others are independent thinkers and aloof, and still others are downright oppositional and obstructionist. These different personality types will determine how trainable a particular dog is. Dogs who are timid and dependent, for example, may have a lot more trouble with *stay* than *come*. "Pulling" breeds, like huskies, may be less disposed to heeling on the leash. Dogs who have never been asked to do anything all their lives are going to be slower to pick up on commands than ones who are used to being trained. Any dog of any age can be successfully trained, but knowing your dog's basic character gives you a big lead.

Know What Motivates Your Senior

The first step in convincing your dog that training is a "plus" is to know what motivates him. Many dogs are motivated primarily by food. In general, the more difficult it is to train your dog, the more likely it is that food will be his prime motivator. If this sounds like your dog, the key is to use treats to encourage success. The more your dog likes food, the lower value the reward will have. For extremely food-oriented pets, one piece of kibble will do the trick. Others may respond only to bits of cheese or freeze-dried liver.

Many senior dogs are most motivated by food during training.

Some dogs will work for petting and praise, others for a little playtime, such as a game of tug, after a successful session. These types of dogs are generally easier to train in the first place. You have probably owned your dog for quite a while and you know him best—you decide what works.

Be Patient

The important thing to keep in mind is that your senior dog is a senior and may have gotten into some bad habits (such as not paying attention to anything you say) over the years. Unfortunately, it takes only a second to develop the habit of "doing one's own thing," but it takes steady application to learn to respond appropriately. Be patient with your senior and he will catch on eventually.

Use Positive Training Techniques

Dogs respond best to positive, reward-based training. Yelling at your dog, jerking his collar, or hitting him is not only cruel but a waste of time, especially for senior dogs. For one thing, many senior dogs don't hear as well as they used to, and your screaming is more likely to puzzle them than startle them into good behavior. In addition, leash jerking can really injure a stiff old neck, and as for striking your dog—that's no way to treat your good friend. Use reward-based training, which uses treats and praise, and your senior will thank you for it.

HOUSETRAINING

If you have adopted an older dog who has spent his life outdoors, it may fall to you to housetrain him. You will be pleased to know that it is usually easier to housetrain an older dog than a puppy because an adult's sphincter muscles are fully developed and he is physically able to "hold it."

How to Housetrain

Housetrain your older dog just as you would a puppy—look for signs that he is ready to "go," such as circling or sniffing, and then hustle him out the door to the designated place. Praise him like crazy when he succeeds, and he will soon learn what is expected of him.

BASIC COMMANDS

No dog is too old to learn good behavior, and while your senior probably already knows his basic commands, it won't hurt to give him a refresher course to keep his mind and body sharp. Working the brain keeps it healthy, and practicing obedience exercises is also good for limbering up old joints. It is also important to maintaining your relationship. If you neglect refresher training for your older dog, he is probably missing some vital interaction with you. (Follow the Version 1 training tips if your senior already knows his basic commands.)

If you never taught your senior dog obedience commands, now is the time to start—this section will show you how. The key is to make the training fun and interesting with praise, petting, and treats. Always end a training exercise on a positive note. (Follow the Version 2 training method if your senior needs to learn his commands from the beginning.)

To housetrain your older dog, look for signs that he has to go, take him outside, and praise him when he succeeds.

Hand Signals for the Hard of Hearing

Senior dogs who are hard of hearing can learn hand signals; they are just as "natural" to them as voice commands. Just as with voice commands, you can make up visual signals that make sense to you. Reward your dog for learning them the same way that you would reward him with obeying voice commands.

Come

Getting your dog to come when called is the most important of all commands. In fact, it's a lifesaver that can protect your dog from being hit by a car, attacked by another dog, or even caught by the dogcatcher (a story I relate later).

Version 1: The Come Refresher

If your dog already knows his basic *come* command but seems bored with it, you may want to spice things up a bit by practicing in a different place or trying out different rewards. For example, instead of the same old piece of cheese, try substituting a different treat—or a walk.

Version 2: Teaching Come for the First Time

To teach the *come* command, start in a quiet room with no distractions. Call your dog, using his name first: "Fido, come!" Speak in a cheerful tone and reward with a small but yummy food treat when he obeys. Of course, you'll be standing very near your senior, no farther than 7 feet (2.1 m) or so. It will help to get his attention with the food treat first. Soon he will come to you quite reliably, at least while you are indoors.

Next, practice outside in a fenced area. You can gradually increase the level of distraction. After a while, you can start giving the reward only sporadically, but always praise your dog when he obeys you.

Sit

The *sit* command is sometimes used to "hold" a nervous or antsy dog in place, or is a prelude to eating or going for a walk. It is probably the easiest of all commands to learn.

Version 1: The Sit Refresher

If your senior already knows this command, he may benefit from learning to sit in different situations such as before meals and walks. You will find that this will calm a nervous senior or make a dominant one more submissive.

Version 2: Teaching Sit for the First Time

Choose a quiet room with no distractions. Say your dog's name and hold a treat right above his nose.

If your senior is hard of hearing, you can use a hand signal to teach him commands such as the *sit*.

SENIOR TALES

"Elwood"

This is the story of Elwood, a very large Bloodhound/Newfoundland mix with a mind of his own. Despite being kept in a "secure yard," the aged Elwood found numerous ways to escape and search for his owner, who was usually in the neighborhood bar. One day, the owner's brother, Rich, was walking down the street and saw Elwood being loaded into the dogcatcher's van. "Hey!" he yelled, "Don't take that dog. That's Elwood! He belongs to my brother!" "Sorry," said the animal control officer. "We're takin' him in." "That's absurd," said Rich. "Elwood!" The dog, who had been looking rather sheepish, looked up. "C'mere, boy—come on!" Elwood's good training came into play, and he whipped his old head around and snapped the leash out of the dog officer's hand, tearing toward Rich.

In the end, the brother's fence was repaired, and Elwood's wandering days were finally over.

Slowly move it backward over his head. He will sit automatically and expectantly. Feed the treat and praise him the instant he sits. This is such an easy skill that most dogs manage to learn it very quickly. After a time, tangible rewards can become intermittent.

Don't push your senior's backside to the ground; this is unnecessarily rough and could even injure your older dog.

Stay

Stay is the long version of the *sit* or *down*. Using it clues your dog in to the fact that he is expected to remain in that position for quite a while. Clever senior dogs take advantage of *stay* by using the opportunity to take a long-awaited nap.

Version 1: The Stay Refresher

As with *sit*, work on using *stay* in different places and situations. In fact, the glory of refreshing the *stay* command is that you can use it while watching your favorite television show until your dog falls asleep. Afterward, you will both be refreshed and ready for action.

Version 2: Teaching Stay for the First Time

Once your dog knows *sit*, the *stay* is the logical follow-up. It's simple. Attach a short lead to his collar, and have your dog sit. Then say "Stay" in a serious tone, and start backing up with your palm out in "stop traffic" position. Move slowly and keep your

Many seniors enjoy lying down because it gives them an opportunity to relax.

eye on your dog. If he gets up, simply and quietly return him to the starting position and try again. When he stays for a few seconds, praise him and give him a treat. Keep practicing, using longer *stay* times and practicing with different variables (such as walking around him). Keep extending the period between the command and the reward. Work toward a five-minute stay time indoors, then move outdoors.

Down

Senior dogs like to spend a lot of down time on their own—napping. However, your goal here is to get your oldster to lie down when requested. Remember, though, that if your senior dog is stiff and arthritic, it's not a lot of fun for him to get up and lie down over and over again on command. Most of the time, a *sit* will work just as well.

Version 1: The Down Refresher

If your dog already knows the *down* command and just needs a refresher, you can try adding distractions to test his ability to stay down when challenged. In the real world, you generally want your dog to stay down because there is something alluring (but possibly dangerous) happening nearby.

Version 2: Teaching Down for the First Time

This is usually an easy command to teach a senior dog because he is ready to lie down anyway. It's getting up that is the problem. Do not overpractice this exercise because it can be hard on a senior's old bones.

To teach this command, ask your dog to sit. Hold a treat close to his nose and gradually lower it to the floor. His nose and eventually the rest of him will follow. Do not push on him, though. Dogs lack a collarbone, and "shoulder assembly" is held in place only by muscles and ligaments. Being forceful can actually dislocate a shoulder.

Walk Nicely on Leash

A dog who walks nicely on leash is a pleasure to take on walks because he won't be pulling on the leash. Walking nicely on a leash does not mean adhering to a rigid heel position, though—it simply means walking calmly on a loose lead. Luckily, senior dogs are more familiar with the world than are their juniors and are less likely to drag you along while they investigate the thrills of the neighborhood. Seniors who walk frequently with their owners are more limber, more successful in their bathroom habits, and happier.

Seniors who walk frequently with their owners are more limber and more successful in their bathroom habits.

Version 1: The Walk Nicely Refresher

If your senior already knows how to walk nicely on leash, spice it up by taking him to new places and having him meet new people. This will also help to keep him well socialized.

Version 2: Teaching Walk Nicely for the First Time

While some dog trainers may disagree, my experience has taught me that the easiest, simplest, and most humane way to quickly get your dog walking calmly at your side is to use a front-loop harness (not a head halter) and just start walking. Dogs, especially old dogs who are set in their ways, much prefer this harness to any head halter or collar.

If you prefer to use a regular collar and leash, simply snap the lead on a flat-buckle collar and place a treat in your hand at hip level. Your dog's nose will gravitate toward the hand and hip, and he will naturally walk along at your side without pulling. You can gradually use the treats less and less often, and soon your dog will be going along beside you with ease.

PROBLEM BEHAVIORS

Older dogs do not suddenly become aggressive, shy, incontinent, or phobic because they are rebelling or undergoing adolescent stress. Always suspect a medical reason for inappropriate behavior that your dog has never displayed before. When puppies urinate on the floor, nip your hands, and run around the house barking, they are exhibiting normal (although undesirable) behavior. When a senior does the same thing, something physical is probably wrong.

Any new undesirable behavior should be checked out by your vet. If she finds nothing wrong, behavior modification is called for.

Aggression

Aggression can be defined as physical violence or the threat of violence, such as biting, snarling, growling, and snapping. Aggression is the most serious problem that any dog can exhibit because it poses a danger to other dogs and people. Fortunately, most senior dogs are not aggressive.

Causes

There are numerous physical causes of aggression in senior dogs, including the following:

- **Brain tumor:** Brain tumors represent as much as 1 to 2 percent of the natural causes of death in dogs and a higher percentage in older dogs. Canine cognitive disorder is also a possibility. (See Chapter 8 to learn more about this disease.)

- **Hormonal diseases:** Some older dogs show a combination of increased appetite and aggression around food. This is a specific marker for certain hormonal diseases, especially Cushing's disease, although diabetes also may produce these changes in some dogs. (See Chapter 8 for more information.)

Warning Signs of Aggression

One of the main warning signs of aggression is the growl, a low-pitched vocalization. The theory behind growling is that big animals are scarier than small ones, and big animals have lower-pitched voices. A growl, therefore, is an attempt to appear more formidable in the face of a threat.

- **Medication:** Certain medications can cause aggression in some dogs. Prednisone and other corticosteroids are famous for this.
- **Pain:** Your dog may be suffering from arthritis or some other ailment that is causing him discomfort.
- **Stress:** Nearly every single instance of aggression, if not physically based, is the result of stress. Some dogs react to stress by withdrawing, some hide, and some bite.

Whatever the cause, don't let sudden unexplained aggression go unnoticed or unexamined. There's something wrong. To help figure out what it is, start keeping a journal of the dog's behavior. In it, take note of the following:

- what triggers the aggression
- to whom it is directed
- how often it occurs (including time of day)
- specifically what happens during the episode, including the dog's posture and your response

Solution

Ask your vet to do a physical examination and to run a general screening blood test, as well as specific tests for Cushing's disease or hypothyroidism if the exam or screening blood tests are normal.

If the trigger is something physical, like pain or disease, your vet can prescribe medication to deal with it. If there is nothing physically wrong with your senior, it's time to get some professional help from a trainer or behaviorist—do not attempt to deal with aggression yourself. Ask your vet to recommend a trainer or behaviorist who specializes in aggression, and follow her advice. Lives—including that of your dog—may be at stake.

Barking

Dogs bark, and it's a normal part of their behavior. It is not possible or desirable to eliminate all barking in our canine friends.

Certified applied animal behaviorists are trained to deal with problem behaviors.

However, sometimes barking exceeds tolerable limits. In that case, it's called "nuisance barking." Old dogs tend to develop a very hoarse, unpleasant-sounding bark.

Causes

- **Boredom:** Boredom and loneliness are the main causes of barking in all dogs. While some calm older dogs fill their empty hours with sleeping more, others resort to barking as a self-soothing device.

- **Canine cognitive disorder (CCD):** If your dog has canine cognitive disorder, he may bark aimlessly for hours. No one knows exactly why, and it is not even clear if these dogs can hear themselves. (See Chapter 8 for information on CCD.)

Solution

In general, older dogs are less likely to bark than are their younger brethren. However, your older dog may still bark when bored and lonely, so the best solution is to bring him inside and give him some attention and stimulation. If you are gone for long hours, try to arrange for a dog walker to come in. That may well help the barking problem, as well as give your dog some needed exercise. If the barking is due to CCD, talk to your vet about an appropriate medication. Please do not resort to electronic antibark collars, which are cruel, frequently "misfire," and have not been shown to be effective.

Begging

Begging can be cute with a puppy, but it is unseemly and annoying in a 12-year-old dog. It makes mealtimes and parties miserable, and the habit that you inadvertently ingrained in your dog in the first place often ends up with him being exiled to a corner of the house. This is not fair to him—you taught him that begging resulted in food as a puppy, so it's up to you to train him out of this habit as a senior.

Causes

- **Hunger:** The truth is that dogs are hungry all the time. They are genetically programmed to

The best way to cure begging is to ignore it and never give in.

be hungry all the time, and there's nothing you can do about that. (Some medications can make dogs ravenous also.) Please do not confuse hunger with malnutrition. It is unlikely that your dog is malnourished, but if you suspect that he is, check with your vet.

- **Your example:** If your senior dog begs at the table, you know that this is a behavior you taught him. As a puppy, his sad and doleful expression melted your heart and you slipped him a bit of toast or chicken. By now the pattern is set—you sit down at the table and so does he.

Solution

What can be done? It's not too late to break the begging cycle, but you're going to have to show a lot more gumption than you have for the past decade. Are you up for it? Here's my advice: Ignore it, and never give in.

You can repair the damage even at this late date. Steel yourself. Keep eating, and don't respond to his begging unless it becomes absolutely intolerable. In that case, put him out of the room. Do this every time, and even the most stubborn beggar will realize that his efforts are futile. Be patient, though; he is doing something that has worked for ten years, and he is not going to stop in a week. If you do wish to give him a bit of your dinner after you eat, you can. But first put all your own dishes away, and give him his portion on his own plate during his regular mealtime.

If your dog is indeed begging because he's too thin and you're not feeding him enough, give him more food—just not from your plate.

Digging

If your senior has never been a digger before, it's unlikely he will start now. However, if he has always been excavating your yard, you still have time to cure the problem, which is simply one of good management.

Causes

- **Boredom:** Digging is an interesting activity for many dogs, and if they have nothing else to occupy their mind, they will dig.
- **Enjoyment:** Many dogs simply enjoy digging for the sake of

Age-Defying Tip

Exercise: The Key to Good Health

Well-trained dogs get more exercise and so get to visit more places. The "more exercise" element will enhance your senior's physical life, and the "more visits" element will add to his mental stimulation. Both will increase his emotional well-being.

Instead of trying to extinguish your senior's digging behavior, redirect his digging to a safe place.

digging. Some breeds, such as terriers, Dachshunds, and huskies, are extremely fond of digging for pleasure.

- **Escape:** For a habitual wanderer, digging provides an escape route under the fence. If you have a dog who is an inveterate escape artist, only complete decrepitude will prevent him from trying to roam. If your dog digs only at the fence line, he's probably looking for a way out.

- **Instinct:** Digging is a natural part of being a dog, and from his point of view, there's nothing wrong with it. In fact, some breeds, such as terriers, Dachshunds, and huskies, have digging firmly embedded in their genes.

- **Provides a Cool Bed:** This is the most common reason why older dogs like to dig—they suffer more from heat. If your dog tends to dig only on warm days, this is probably the reason.

Going Professional

If your dog's problem behaviors stump you, it may be time to visit a professional. The top of the line is a veterinary behaviorist. A veterinary behaviorist has a degree in veterinary medicine and has gone through an internship and behavioral residency training program. Residencies are two or three years long (depending on the resident's experience and coursework) and are conducted under an already boarded veterinary behaviorist.

The problem is that there are very few diplomated veterinary behaviorists at the present time in the United States, although many vets do specialize in behavior issues without having the formal credentials of "veterinary behaviorist." Veterinarians who specialize in animal behavior but who are not diplomates are referred to as "veterinary animal behaviorists."

Another possibility is to seek the advice of a certified applied animal behaviorist, someone certified to practice by the Animal Behavior Society (ABS). These people are well suited to handle nonmedical behavioral issues. Their psychology background makes them ideal when it comes to managing disturbed dogs who have suffered psychological trauma.

Solution

Don't try to extinguish your senior's digging behavior, and don't punish him. Punishment for natural behavior simply makes dogs neurotic. Instead, redirect his digging to a safe place. That safe place will be his very own earthbox! (Your senior will really appreciate this during the "dog days" of summer.) To make an earthbox, take a corner of your backyard and dig up the earth in it, making it soft and inviting. You can enclose it if you like with wood, like a sandbox, to keep the dirt in. Bury some treats in the earth, and start digging around in it yourself. Your dig-happy dog will soon catch on to the fun. When you see him digging elsewhere, simply lead him to the earthbox, and try digging along with him.

To reduce the need to dig, keep your dog occupied. For older dogs, that might just mean joining you on the couch for an afternoon of soap operas.

If your dog is trying to escape, you'll need to make sure that he can't. Bury the bottom of your fence at least 1 foot (0.3 m) underground to keep him safe. If your dog is not neutered, have it done—it will reduce his desire to roam.

Housetraining Issues

If your previously housetrained dog suddenly loses or "forgets" his housetraining, there is a reason for it—usually physical but possibly psychological.

If your older dog suddenly "forgets" his housetraining, have him checked out by a vet.

Causes

- **You:** You may be leaving your dog alone too long. This is the most common reason that a dog "forgets" his housetraining. His aging sphincter just can't hold it as long as before.

- **Canine cognitive disorder (CCD):** This condition affects a large number of seniors and many behaviors. (See Chapter 8.)

- **Spay incontinence:** Older spayed females may have lost muscle tone and begun to "leak."

- **Medications:** Certain medications, like prednisone, can result in increased thirst, which leads to increased urination. If your dog is confined too long, he won't be able to hold it.

Pheromones

Mother dogs naturally secrete a pheromone that calms their puppies. You can purchase this pheromone to help to calm a nervous or fearful dog. Some products come in a spray, while others emit the substance, kind of like an air freshener.

Cleaning Up Accidents

If it's fresh urine, clean the rug with a good carpet shampoo. However, if the urine has penetrated through the rug to the pad beneath, it's unlikely that you'll be able to remove it completely. Purchase an odor remover that contains enzymes to break down the odor-causing compounds in urine and feces. Follow the directions carefully, and let the cleaner soak in as deeply as the urine itself.

Solution

If your older dog suddenly "forgets" his housetraining, don't assume that the problem is behavioral—there are many medical causes. Have your dog checked out by a vet.

If no medical problems have been found and you are increasing your senior's opportunities to relieve himself, you may need to consult a behaviorist. If you have adopted an older dog who is not used to being in a house, train him just the same as you would a puppy: with a routine, patience, and watchfulness. When you take him outside for a potty break, watch him carefully. Take him on a leash to the same spot every time. When he does what is required, praise him extravagantly. You can then play with him briefly as a reward before going back in. Of course, you'll have a longer playtime later.

If your dog makes a mistake, remove all traces of the urine with an enzyme cleaner. If you don't, he will be tempted to return to the same spot.

Dogs who have become incontinent for any reason may profit from disposable diapers of soft absorbent cotton or male dog "wraps" to stop leakage. The wraps usually have an all-around elastic waistband plus adjustable Velcro bands to give your dog a snug, comfortable fit.

Noise Phobias

Dogs are not generally fond of noises (except their own barking). This may have something to do with their history as wild creatures out on the plains, when thunder signaled dangerous lightning. Sure enough, thunderphobia is extremely common generations later.

Thunderphobia almost never appears in puppies but becomes increasingly common in older dogs, especially in herding and hunting breeds—dogs most likely to be caught in a storm. Dogs with thunderphobia show extreme signs of terror, such as pacing, panting, whining, hiding, and even trying desperately to escape.

Unfortunately, noise phobias do seem to become worse over time, and eventually, dogs with one kind of phobia—like thunderphobia—may come to fear any loud noise: vacuum cleaners, fireworks, gunshots, and the like.

Causes

Sometimes thunderphobia occurs after a single terrifying incident, such as a particularly violent storm, while at other times it seems to come on more gradually, with no precipitating event known.

Solution

If your older dog has a noise phobia, get him checked out by a vet to make sure that there is nothing else wrong with him.

Many dogs with thunderphobia respond well to melatonin or dog-appeasing pheromones. In some cases, you can use "white noise" like the television or

Most senior dogs are not fond of loud noises.

talk radio (which works better than music) to cover the offending sound, or you can try to counter-condition your senior by gradually exposing him to increasing levels of the offending noise. Often, it is just as useful to let him hide in a safe place. In any case, don't try to soothe him with coddling and petting. That will only serve to reinforce in his mind the fact that something very dangerous is going on. Be positive and cheerful—maybe it will rub off!

Separation Anxiety

Canine separation anxiety is a behavioral disorder characterized by a dog who panics or becomes terribly upset and nervous when left alone. Such dogs are pathologically attached to their owners.

Dogs with separation anxiety are destructive and may attempt to flee the home—some have been known to go through windows! This behavior is a mark of a dog's fear, not some attempt to get revenge on his owners, although it may seem like that.

A dog with separation anxiety may be a "Velcro dog" while you are home, following you everywhere. He will become anxious at signs of your leaving and may begin to whine and cry almost immediately (and without ceasing) when you do go. He may yip in a high-pitched tone, defecate or urinate in the home, destroy property, and refuse to eat in your absence. (These behaviors begin within 30 minutes after you leave. If the dog displays these behaviors while you are home, he probably does not have separation anxiety.) A dog with separation anxiety becomes overenthusiastic upon your return.

Causes

- **Canine cognitive dysfunction (CCD):** Canine cognitive dysfunction seems to affect many aspects of a dog's behavior, such as his confidence and independence. (See Chapter 8.)

- **Prior living situation:** Dogs who exhibit separation anxiety were typically acquired by the owner after three months of age or before six weeks of age; were orphaned or hand raised; were obtained from a shelter or pound; or belonged to several different owners.

Solution

To help your dog deal with separation anxiety, desensitize him to your leaving. Do this by first imitating your daily departure routine, including all the prep work. Then leave. Give your dog a very special, high-value treat that he gets only while you are absent from the home—something stuffed with good cheese or even meat. Don't make a big deal out of leaving. Just say "Good-bye, Fido," and take off. Come back in 15 seconds—before he knows what hit him. Praise him if he has been quiet and nondestructive. Then leave again, and continue this routine until your dog stops barking. Over a period of weeks, you can leave for longer and longer times. Don't try to do this too fast, though—expect it to take a long time, even months.

Never punish a dog for having separation anxiety. That will only make it worse. Also, do not crate a dog with separation anxiety unless you literally have no other choice or unless you know that the dog regards the crate as a safe place, because it usually increases the feelings of panic. A panicky dog can tear out his nails or break teeth attempting to remove himself from the crate. An older, at-risk senior

> **⚔ Senior Moment ⚔**
>
> **Overpraising Your Senior**
>
> It's possible to overpraise and overreward your dog. If you are constantly handing out treats and praise, he will no longer regard them as rewards and they will become useless training tools. So use praise as a "reward" when your dog obeys your commands. If you use food as a reward, don't hand out a dog biscuit every time your senior looks inquiringly at you.

A dog with separation anxiety may refuse to eat in your absence.

could even go into bloat and die, because one of the primary precipitating factors for bloat is stress.

If desensitization is not working, it's time to see the vet. She may prescribe medication for CCD or may try clomipramine to treat the separation anxiety directly. At present, clomipramine (used once or twice a day) is the only FDA-approved drug for the treatment of separation anxiety in dogs. However, some other human anti-anxiety medications also have been used. Drugs are meant to be used as a supplement to training, however, not as a substitute for training.

Training is to your dog what reading and game playing are to people: educational, fun, challenging, and essential to an enriched life. Depriving your dog of the opportunity to learn and be part of your life is not what he signed up for.

Chapter 6

ACTIVITIES FOR THE SENIOR DOG

Just because your dog has reached a certain age does not mean that he can't take or continue to take an active part in your life—or even participate in a few activities on his own. In fact, older dogs, because they are generally calm, sensible, and trained, may make much better traveling companions and competitors than heedless youngsters.

TRAVELING WITH YOUR SENIOR

For many people, a vacation simply isn't a vacation without their best pal. If this is you, take a few simple steps to make your trip safe and enjoyable. Just because your dog is older doesn't mean that you can't take him with you.

To make the most of any experience, it's important to be prepared. The simple steps listed here can save you aggravation, time, money, or even heartache when traveling together.

- Get a health checkup for your dog within ten days before a trip, and ask your vet to provide a certificate stating that your dog is in good health and up-to-date on vaccines. Take the record with you, especially if you are crossing state lines.

- Make sure that your dog is on a flea/tick preventive.

- Make sure that your dog has proper identification tags in addition to any

The safest way for your senior to travel by car is in a secured crate or seat belted in the back seat.

microchipping or tattooing.

- Bring your pet's favorite dog food, bedding, leashes, toys, medication, bowls, crate, bottles of water, pooper scooper or plastic bag, and extra food and water.

Car Travel

The safest way for your old dog to travel is in a secured crate or seat belted in the back seat. (Dogs in the front seat are at risk of being killed if the airbag is deployed.) You can even purchase a seat belt made especially for dogs. If your dog is not secured in the car, he could climb into your lap while you are driving, or if you stop suddenly, he could be injured.

Although dogs love to travel with their noses hanging out the window to catch the scents on the breeze, don't allow your pet to do this. All kinds of dirt and debris can come flying along and catch your dog in the eye—pieces of asphalt, bits of wood, rocks, you name it. A shard of glass can blind him. And of course, never leave your dog unattended in the car.

If your dog is prone to motion sickness and you have no medication for him, try ginger snaps. They work amazingly well to help an upset tummy. If the motion sickness is due to nervousness, consider purchasing a product that contains pheromones. Just spray it in his crate or on the back seat to help calm him down.

Airplane Travel

Older dogs are quite able to handle flying if they are healthy. The only really safe place for your pet is in the cabin with you, but if your dog is too big to fit under the seat in his carrier, you are usually out of luck. If you have no choice other than to transport your dog in the cargo hold, the ASPCA

SENIOR TALES

"Mellie"

Jean remembers, "I went on vacation when Mellie was well into her 13th year. I left her at home with a pet sitter she knew and loved who spent the night with her and came in to check on her several times a day. The night I returned from vacation, I let myself in the front door and found Mellie in her favorite spot in the family room. When she saw me, she went nuts and showed more energy than she had in quite some time. She did my heart good greeting me with so much enthusiasm.

"It was obvious from her welcome home dance that she missed me almost as much as I missed her. However, being the independent girl that she was, after greeting me and getting some extra love and treats, Mellie went back to bed in her favorite spot downstairs. Normally she would have come upstairs to get in bed with me sometime during the night so that she could get her good morning snuggles first thing in the morning.

"I woke up the next morning and realized that Mellie hadn't joined me, so I immediately ran downstairs thinking that something must be wrong with my old girl. The only thing wrong was that Mellie had forgotten I was home! She was just hanging out downstairs. I called her name, she turned around and saw me, and then she proceeded to perform the exact same, very enthusiastic welcome home dance she did the night before. Her senior moment certainly made my morning!"

recommends that you follow the air travel guidelines provided on their website: www. aspca.org/traveltips.

Some airlines suggest that dogs who are more than seven and a half years of age receive an extensive health screening, including kidney and liver screens, or possibly an electrocardiogram, before flying.

It is not a good idea to give your dog tranquilizers before an airplane trip because they can interfere with breathing and temperature regulation at high altitudes.

Senior-Friendly Accommodations

Before you take off into wild, wonderful vacationland, make sure that you have pet-friendly accommodations lined up. Look online to find extensive lists of hotels, motels, cabins, condos, resorts, bed and breakfasts, beaches, RV parks, and campgrounds that will welcome your well-behaved senior. Some of the best sites include www.dogfriendly. com, www.petfriendlytravel.com, and www.welcomepet.com.

A pet sitter can care for your dog while you are away for an extended period.

If Your Senior Can't Join You

It is not always possible, or even desirable, to bring your dog along on your travels. Senior dogs especially may prefer to remain behind. Some older dogs find traveling scary and stressful, especially if they are feeble or disabled. And while you may enjoy visiting your Aunt Enid's Rottweiler, don't assume that your ancient toy Poodle will find it an equally pleasant experience. For some dogs, this means a pet sitter or a kennel. For other dogs, whose owner is at work, this means a day care facility. Let's look at these options.

Pet Sitters

For most dogs and people, a pet sitter offers tremendous advantages. You will not have to worry about transporting your dog to an unfamiliar kennel. Even more important, your older dog will not be exposed to strange dogs and whatever contagious diseases they may be carrying. Your dog will have his regular bed, food, and even routine. Equally nice for you is the fact that most pet sitters will pick up your mail, water your plants, and even straighten up for you. And simply having someone there on occasion can be a crime deterrent.

But how to choose? Check with your veterinarian, who can probably recommend someone. The best pet sitter will offer a service contract with specified fees and will have a vet on call for emergency services. Before you sign anything, ask the sitter to come by your home, and evaluate her interaction with your dog. Your dog's response to her will tell you quite a bit.

Kennels

Sometimes a pet sitter is not an option. In this case, a good boarding kennel attuned to a senior's needs may be your best choice. Get recommendations from your friends or vet, and visit the facility before committing. Be sure to book ahead. Most kennels are swamped all the time. Here are some indications that the kennel you're considering is a good one:

- **It's licensed and inspected.** Ask for proof. Good kennels are accredited by the American Boarding Kennel Association (ABKA).

- **It's clean.** Check out the walls, floors, and food bowls. Food should be kept in airtight, pest-proof containers.

- **It's reasonably quiet.** Although a kennel will never be as quiet as a library, you don't want your dog subjected to 24 hours of nonstop barking either. He may become stressed with the noise—or he may pick up the habit himself.

- **It's spacious.** Some kennels provide individual runs for each dog, while others bring dogs into a common area for play. (This is good for socialization but can pose health risks.) Discuss how the kennel plans to ensure your dog's safe exercise. If you don't want your dog associating with others, make that clear.

- **It's climate controlled.** This is not a luxury but a necessity for an old dog who has more difficulty regulating his body temperature than a young dog has.

- **It's well ventilated.** Your dog requires fresh, clean air. A well-ventilated kennel keeps the air from stagnating.

- **It has a vet on call.** Many kennels employ veterinary technicians on staff. All staff should be trained in CPR and basic first-aid techniques.

- **It has both indoor and outdoor runs.** Dogs enjoy fresh air, but when it rains or is bitterly cold, your senior deserves to get his exercise indoors, in climate-controlled comfort.

- **It's secure.** If your dog is an escape artist, let the kennel manager know in advance.

- **It's safe.** The kennel should be equipped with fire alarms, sprinkler systems, and double doors.

- **It provides good bedding.** Most kennels will allow you to bring your dog's own bed for him if you'd like.

- **It separates the animals.** Good kennels do not allow nose-to-nose contact between animals, both for fear of spreading disease and to prevent barrier fighting. Does the kennel have adequate quarantine facilities? This is an important consideration if a boarded dog should develop symptoms of a contagious disease.

- **It has Sunday hours.** Many boarding kennels are closed on Sunday, and pets are unavailable for pickup. Sunday, of course, is the very day when most people want to pick up their pets.

Many kennels offer grooming services, special playtimes, private rooms, obedience classes, swimming, and other activities for your dog, usually at an extra fee. Some kennels will allow you to board two of your dogs together. Be sure to inquire.

⤙ Senior Moment ⤚

Maintaining Your Dog's Schedule

While on a trip, try to keep to your normal feeding and walking schedules as much as possible. This reduces your dog's stress and will lessen the likelihood of a housetraining accident.

Good day care centers put dogs of similar size and temperament together.

Day Care

Doggy day care is a kind of boarding facility for dogs whose owners are at work. Dogs are social creatures who do much better when they have human and (usually) canine company. But most people have to work for long hours a day. For many, the answer lies in doggy day care. Day care can be especially important if your senior dog is on a medication that may need to be given several times a day.

You have a lot of choices when it comes to canine day care. Some places offer nothing more than rudimentary runs and water, while others are state-of-the-art. Many include basic obedience classes, grooming services, and even canine "spas." Climate-controlled play areas, wading pools, and doggy gyms are commonplace. A few even have "petcams" on at all times so that you can observe your dog from afar (and make sure that he is getting everything he deserves).

Good day care facilities also expect your dog to be up to date on his vaccinations (especially bordetella) and on a regular flea/tick preventive. You may be asked to fill out

Exercise and Safety

Exercise helps your oldster dog maintain muscle tone and keep his heart strong and his digestive system in good working order. It even improves his outlook on life. Your older dog enjoys walks and mild exercise, but please keep him from running on hard surfaces and jumping from high places. Think low impact, and include warm-up and cool down periods. This can help to prevent arthritis. Time the walks, if possible, so that you will avoid the worst of the heat and cold.

a questionnaire about your dog's temperament, level of training, and preferences. He also may be evaluated before being accepted into a day care program.

Before signing up, you should be looking around and doing some evaluating on your own. Many of the same criteria apply here as those relating to kennels. Visit the day care facility before you enroll your dog. It should obviously be clean, nice smelling, and well cared for. It also should be safe. Safety measures may include double doors or other "decompression zones" to keep dogs from escaping. Most good day cares have a connection with a nearby vet in case an emergency happens. Good day care centers put dogs of similar size together and separate overly boisterous animals. Regulations should be written down for your perusal.

Take time to meet with and interview the staff, and ask specifically what the staff–dog ratio is. (It shouldn't be more than one staff person per ten dogs.) Ask the staff what its procedure is when introducing new dogs, and if they have special provisions for seniors who may be more interested in a quiet nap than a playgroup session. Observe staff members' interactions with the dogs as well. They should be attentive, friendly, and knowledgeable about their charges.

Good day care facilities willingly provide references.

ORGANIZED SPORTS AND ACTIVITIES

Older dogs can continue to compete in organized sports and activities well into their golden years. Aging is a subjective thing, and if your dog has been checked out thoroughly by your vet, there is no reason why he can't continue to perform. The famous sled dog Balto was pulling and racing sleds well into his teens!

Many performance events have special classes just for veteran dogs, and others, such as tracking, are physically undemanding enough so that dogs of all ages can enjoy them. You should, of course, use your common sense. It would be ridiculous to take a 13-year-old couch potato and decide to make an agility champion out of him. Match your dog to a moderately paced, low-stress event that he shows an interest in and enjoys. As a senior, he has earned the right to choose his own level of involvement.

Agility

Canine agility trials are really obstacle courses for dogs. Agility gives your senior a chance to get his exercise, experience mental challenges, and have fun all at the same time.

Many organizations allow veterans ages six and older to compete at lower jump heights. However, this demanding sport should be reserved for dogs in top condition because the running and jumping involved can be hard on old joints.

The United States Dog Agility Association (USDAA) and North American Dog Agility Council (NADAC) both provide "veteran classes."

Many agility organizations allow veterans aged six and older to compete at lower jump heights.

Older dogs with an established show career often continue to enjoy the sport.

Canine Good Citizen Test

Once your dog has mastered the essentials of training, you can try to "put a title" on him. Any dog, purebred or not, is eligible to apply for the AKC's Canine Good Citizen test, a program that began in 1989. The purpose of this noncompetitive test is to certify that your dog is well behaved and gentle in public. No dog is too old to be a good citizen!

Your senior will be tested on the following ten skills:

Test 1: Accepting a friendly stranger.

Test 2: Sitting politely for petting.

Test 3: Appearance and grooming.

Test 4: Out for a walk (walk on a loose leash).

Test 5: Walking through a crowd.

Test 6: "Sit" and "down" on command; stay" in place.

Test 7: Coming when called.

Test 8: Reaction to another dog.

Test 9: Reactions to distractions.

Test 10: Supervised separation.

All tests are performed using a leash. The evaluator will provide a 20-foot (6.1-m) lead for the *down/stay* exercise, but owners should bring a comb or brush for the grooming exercise.

Conformation

Conformation classes are the beauty events of the show dog world, and while almost no one suddenly decides to start showing an older dog, there is no reason why an older dog cannot continue an established show career. While you may not want to subject your oldster to the commotion of such a major event, most breed specialty shows have veteran events that are just for senior dogs. This is your chance to get your dog out into the wide world and show off what excellent care you have taken of him over the years.

Regular conformation classes are for purebred dogs only, but many humane societies and rescues offer "fun shows" in which your dog can stand out as the "prettiest," "best groomed," "best mix," and even "best kisser." Many also have special classes for senior dogs.

Every breed club has specialty events at which the "veteran classes" are almost always the most popular with the crowd. It is truly wonderful to see these noble oldsters parading around their old haunts.

SENIOR TALES

"Sadie"

Gwen relates, "Sadie has always loved attention and she is a sweetheart, so she became a therapy dog. She gets all the attention that she loves and deserves from the senior home we visit. We mostly go to the skilled nursing ward, where the residents have difficulty getting around or are bedridden. They love Sadie there, and she gets so excited when we go through the security gate. She'll start barking and continue until I can get her leash on and take her out of the car. Then, when we get inside, her tail wags excitedly and she goes to each room to let the residents love on her and feed her treats."

Obedience

Obedience is another event at which senior dogs can really strut their stuff. This sport tests the training of dogs as they work through a series of exercises on command. Competitive obedience pushes dogs beyond simple *sit*, *stay*, and *heel* commands, although they must have these skills too.

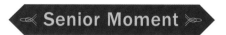
Several levels of competition exist, from basic commands to scent discrimination and directed retrieves over jumps. If your senior is biddable and physically able, there is no reason why he cannot pursue an obedience title, just like his younger counterparts. Obedience is really just a mental sport.

The AKC has obedience classes for purebreds, but if you have a mixed breed and want to participate, don't despair. Check out the American Mixed Breed Obedience Registration (AMBOR).

Rally Obedience

Rally obedience is similar to classical obedience but more interactive, easier, and as many will tell you, more fun. In rally, there are numbered stations; each station is a sign with instructions that tell the handler what skill the dog needs to display at that point. You are permitted to talk to your dog throughout the course, which is not allowed in regular obedience, as well as give hand signals, which is great for older deaf dogs.

Many kennel clubs and breed clubs that offer rally obedience have special classes just for veterans.

Therapy Work

While in days of yore dogs were most likely to accompany their owners hunting or herding sheep, today many are involved in more humane work: visiting the sick, depressed, imprisoned, and elderly. Some animals and their handlers are specially trained, but in most cases, the dog simply needs to be quiet, friendly, and calm. Their very presence makes a difference in people's lives.

Older dogs make wonderful therapy animals. They tend to be quieter and are less apt to shock an elderly or ill person with sudden movements than a wild puppy is. You can get involved in a caring project that brings people and their pets together with residents of hospitals, nursing homes, schools, rehabilitation centers, and other places.

Check with your local hospital or other facility to see if a therapy program is in your area, and ask how you can sign up your older dog.

Tracking

Tracking is a superb event for senior dogs, and dogs of any age can learn to do it. In this event, a dog uses his nose to find a leather glove or other article with a human scent. A "tracklayer" lays the track by walking along and leaving the article. This is a slow-paced, healthy outdoor activity that your senior will really enjoy. The only equipment you need is a tracking harness, a glove, and a 30- to 40-foot (9.1- to 12.2-m) lead.

Most tracking events are held by the AKC, so your dog must be a purebred to participate. The United Kennel Club (UKC) also offers tracking events. The best way to learn the sport is to get involved with a dog club that has tracking members.

JUST FOR FUN: NONORGANIZED ACTIVITIES

Not everyone enjoys organized events with schedules, rules, and timetables—at least not every day. If you're a free spirit or maybe just want to have alone time with your dog, you can flee the whirlwind of show clusters and head for the woods and trails.

Camping

As long as you're not planning on a rigorous hike up jagged and dangerous mountain paths or through steamy, alligator-infested jungles, a quiet weekend camping trip is just the thing to get you and your senior dog away from suburbia to experience the glories of nature.

Before you go, though, get your dog checked for any incipient health problems, and make sure that his vaccinations are up to date. Bring his rabies certificate with you, just in case.

His identification tags should include not just your home contact information but also the name of the park and campground with their telephone information. After all, if you lose your dog around the campsite, it won't help if the finder keeps calling your house back in New Jersey.

- **Know your senior's limits.** If you're planning to do some hiking, keep it within your senior's capacities.

One of the simplest and best-loved activities for the senior dog is a simple walk.

Condition your dog (and yourself) before you make the trip. While hiking, check your dog's footpads carefully to make sure that he's not getting sore.

- **Keep your dog on the trail.** Letting him trot off into the underbrush could result in a very nasty surprise—one that has fangs or stingers.

- **Dispose of waste properly.** If your dog eliminates, bury the mess on the side of the trail or tote it along in a small plastic bag until you reach a trash receptacle.

- **Follow the rules.** Most campgrounds permit pets on a leash, but there are always exceptions. Call ahead to make sure. And if your dog is a barker, camp away from others.

- **Bring a first-aid kit, plenty of food, dishes, and extra leashes.** If your dog is in great shape, he may be able to help carry some of his own things with a special dog backpack. If your older dog is a toy breed, it's not too much to expect you to carry him—dog totes are available!

- **Pack extra water.** Even the most pristine mountain water can be full of giardia or other pathogens.

Walking

One of the simplest and most enjoyable of all activities is the classic dog walk. Dogs never get tired of them, and even the oldest dog enjoys a gentle stroll around the block in addition to his "bathroom breaks."

Because older dogs are temperature sensitive, schedule walks (if possible) for early mornings and evenings in hot weather and in the warmer parts of the day in winter. As your dog ages, he needs as many walks as before because his bladder isn't what it used to be, but the walks need not be so long nor so fast. These are his golden years, so let him sniff the roses if he wants to. And don't neglect your older dog if you have a youngster who needs vigorous playtime. If you head for the dog park or even your own yard on a summer day, park your senior under a shady tree with plenty of water. He will enjoy resting and watching and will still feel a part of things.

Age-Defying Tip

Keep Your Dog on the Leash

When out hiking with your dog, keep him on a leash. A city dog may find a porcupine or skunk simply fascinating and not recognize the ominous rattle of a diamondback for what it is. Make your dog's life longer by keeping the leash fairly short.

Take some time to relax with your senior dog.

I will tell you what my favorite activity with my senior dog, Miles, is: We head out to the backyard. I get the hammock; Miles gets his special portable dog bed. I get the iced tea; Miles gets cold water in a bowl and a chew toy. I bring my book; Miles forgets his, so I read to him. Strangely enough, we both like the very same books! Admittedly, Miles falls asleep in the warm sun before I finish. I know he is dreaming of the old days—the race across the field after the rabbits he could never quite catch, the wind in his fur. The wind has died to a gentle breeze now, but it still tickles his fur, and I daresay he is having as good a time as ever. I know I am.

In short, your older dog neither needs nor wants ceaseless activity. He wants your love and your company. Take some down time with your dog, and dust off that book!

⫸ *Chapter 7* ⫷

WELLNESS AND PREVENTIVE CARE

Most senior dogs have great genes—that's how they got to be seniors in the first place. But as he ages, your dog depends on you to help him keep that healthy glow. Owners who pay attention to their dog's health needs year-round can look forward to many wonderful and active years with their best friend.

GERIATRIC VETERINARY VISITS

Because dogs age many times faster than humans do, major health changes can develop in a short amount of time. That's why a wellness exam every six months is essential to your senior's well-being.

Choosing a Geriatric Vet

If you already have a vet you know and trust, there is no need to change your primary practitioner. Of course, you may need to see a specialist for a particular problem, but most good vets are used to older pets. However, if you are uncertain, ask if anyone on the staff has received additional education in geriatric veterinary medicine.

If your older dog is a new adoptee and you don't have a vet, here are some major considerations:

- **Location:** While the nearest vet may not be the best one, you also don't want to travel an hour when a good vet is ten minutes away. In an emergency, a few minutes of travel time can make the difference between life and death.

- **Hours:** Check to see if the office is open at hours convenient to you. Places that are closed weekends and evenings should have a backup office.

Your vet and her staff should be friendly and knowledgeable about geriatric dogs.

- **The Facility:** The vet's office should be clean and its staff friendly and knowledgeable about geriatric dogs.

- **Equipment and Procedures:** While not every vet office is able to perform every medical procedure possible, many can do X-rays, ultrasound, acupuncture, laser surgery, behavioral therapy, endoscopy, electrocardiograms, and blood work.

When to Start Those Geriatric Checkups

Take your healthy senior to the vet for his first geriatric workup on something like the following schedule:

Weight	Age to Begin Geriatric Workup
Less than 15 pounds (6.8 kg)	9 to 11 years
16 to 50 pounds (7.3 to 22.7 kg)	7 to 9 years
51 to 80 pounds (23.1 to 36.3 kg)	6 to 8 years
More than 80 pounds (36.3 kg)	4 to 6 years

Of course, if your senior shows any signs of illness, he should go to the vet at once, schedule or no schedule. Here are some classic danger signs:

- aggression or other behavioral changes
- black, tarry stools
- breathing difficulty or coughing
- changes in the appearance of the eyes (red, inflamed, cloudy, bulging)
- diarrhea or vomiting
- difficulty moving
- difficulty urinating
- extreme lethargy

- fever
- increased appetite with no weight gain
- increased thirst and urination without an increase in activity level
- loss of hearing or vision (or hypersensitivity to either)
- protruding rectum
- severe pain
- seizures
- sudden lameness
- trauma or accident
- sudden loss of weight or appetite
- unexplained lump or bump

At your senior's physical exam, the vet will check his blood pressure and heart rate.

How to Collect a Urine Sample

The easiest method of collecting a urine sample is the old "free catch" method, in which you take your dog for a walk and slip a clean plastic container underneath when he lifts his leg (or she squats). Try to collect the urine midstream—begin collecting the sample several seconds or more after your pet begins to urinate. If you must wait a few hours before going to the vet, cover the container with the urine and keep it in the refrigerator. If for some reason you can't manage that, the urine can be collected at the clinic with a urinary catheter. In many cases, the vet may use a procedure called cystocentesis, a procedure in which a needle is inserted directly into the bladder. Vets often prefer this option because it provides an uncontaminated sample.

What Happens at a Geriatric Screening

A geriatric screening of your dog may include: (1) a thorough hands-on physical exam; (2) blood tests; (3) electrocardiogram; (4) urinalysis; (5) fecal exam; (6) specialized tests, depending on your dog's health history.

Physical Exam

A good physical exam for older dogs usually includes a dental check, weight check, heartworm antigen test, rectal exam (to check the inner pelvic area, lymph nodes, colon lining, and prostate), and ophthalmic exam (to check for cataracts, glaucoma, and dry eye). Also, the vet will record your dog's blood pressure and heart rate.

Blood Tests

Blood tests, including a complete blood count (CBC) and blood chemistry panel, may also be ordered. A blood cell count evaluates the blood cells themselves and is a test recommended for dogs with complaints such as fever, vomiting, weakness, pale gums, or loss of appetite. It also gives information on hydration status, anemia, infection, blood clotting ability, and the immune system's ability to respond to infections. A blood chemistry panel identifies warning signs of several liver, kidney, and hormonal diseases. Not every blood panel tests for every condition; your vet will select which tests she is most interested in seeing.

Electrocardiogram

The electrocardiogram measures heart function and may be required if your vet detects an abnormal heartbeat during the physical examination. The dog's heart function is recorded as a linear graph on a sheet of paper. New technology makes this a snap in a well-equipped vet's office because wires are no longer needed.

Urinalysis

Your vet also may want to perform a urinalysis, especially if you have noticed warning signs such as a change in the color, odor, or amount of your senior's urine; a change in urinary habits; difficulty urinating; or any blood in the urine.

Urine is more than a waste product—it's a clue to your dog's health. Odd as it sounds, there's a lot that you can learn from dog urine. Healthy urine is a clear yellow with a characteristic doggy urine smell. A healthy dog will develop a particular pattern of urinating the same frequency and amount each day, and a wise owner will note when the urination pattern changes or when the urine looks or smells different. When that happens, it may be time to collect a fresh sample and take it to your vet.

The concentration, color, clarity, and microscopic examination of the urine sample can provide diagnostic information about several body systems. Your vet will check the sediment in the urine for increased white blood cells (possibly indicating a bladder infection, quite common in females). Diabetic dogs may have increased glucose in the urine. The vet also will measure the specific gravity of the urine—an abnormal level can indicate abnormal kidney function. Crystals in the urine may indicate the presence of bladder stones, which can be caused by dietary or liver problems.

If your senior has been ill, take him back to the vet for a "recheck exam" to see what progress, if any, he has made.

Fecal Exam

Regular fecal tests are important. They reveal the eggs of internal parasites such as roundworms, hookworms, and whipworms. These are too small to be seen with the naked eye, but your vet can perform a "fecal flotation" that makes the eggs float up and collect on a microscope slide.

Specialized Tests

Today's vets can take advantage of many high-tech procedures to see what is going on with your dog. Here are some of the most common:

- **Radiograph or X-ray:** The most familiar of these tests is the radiograph or

X-ray, especially if your dog has a history of certain heart, lung, kidney, or gastrointestinal trouble, or if he has had cancer. The X-ray machine projects X-rays through the patient onto X-ray-sensitive film. X-rays are most useful for examining the chest, bones, joints, and abdomen. Depending on the type of X-ray and the temperament of your dog, he may need to be anesthetized for this procedure.

- **Ultrasound:** This test uses high-frequency sound waves to detect problems in the heart, spleen, liver, and other soft organs. It is great for older dogs because it gives cross-sectional images without the dog having to go under general anesthesia. The procedure takes less than half an hour and has no dangers or side effects. One special form of ultrasound is echocardiology, which gives an excellent picture of the patient's heart.

- **CAT Scan:** Another tool is the CAT (computerized axial tomography) scan. With this test, a very thin beam of X-rays passes through a cross-section of the body in a rotational manner. The beam can be adjusted to show very specific image "slices," like the skull one section at a time. A computer also can use the scan to create a three-dimensional image. The CAT scan is useful in determining subtle variations in tissue. This technology is often used in cases of compressive spinal disorders, abnormal tissue growth, and areas of the head, nose, or ears. Animals must be anesthetized for this procedure because they must lie very still.

- **MRI:** The MRI (magnetic resonance imaging) test uses radio waves and powerful magnetic fields to create images. It creates a vibration in the fluid found in the body, which in turn emits a radio signal. A receptor coil produces a cross-sectional image of the water content found in the body's tissues. Bones are not shown (they contain too little water), but this imaging gives the best views of soft tissues like the liver or brain. It also gives the most precise pictures. Animals must be anesthetized for this procedure because they need to lie still.

All these diagnostic tools require special training, and many are expensive, cumbersome, and unsuited to an all-purpose veterinary practice, which may have only an X-ray machine. If your dog needs a special test, your vet may refer you to a specialist.

The Recheck Exam

While most dog owners are pretty good about getting their senior

⊰ **Senior Moment** ⊱

Urine Analysis

Your senior's urine sample can provide the vet with diagnostic information about several body systems.

to the vet when he shows signs of illness, some tend to skip the all-important "recheck exam." If your senior has been ill, the veterinarian needs to assess the progress (or lack of) that your dog has made since the initial diagnosis. Even if your dog seems to be better, your vet may want to recheck blood or urine to make sure. Dogs with chronic diseases are most in need of this follow-up care, and in the long run it will save you money and keep your dog healthier.

NORMAL VALUES FOR YOUR SENIOR

The only way to know if there is something wrong with your dog is to know when things are normal. This section provides some baseline normal values for senior dogs. Some variation is not uncommon, and an "abnormal" value does not necessarily mean that your dog is ill. However, it does bear, at the very least, looking into further.

Breath

A healthy senior dog won't have bad breath unless he's just eaten something awful. Most of the time bad breath means bad teeth, but certain kinds of bad breath can alert you to other problems. A sweet smell may suggest diabetes, a urine-like odor may indicate a kidney disorder, a foul smell may point to liver disease, and a sour or rancid smell might mean that there's a problem with the intestines. Always get bad breath checked out by your vet.

Breathing Rate

When breathing normally, the chest expands upon inhalation. If the abdomen, rather than the chest, expands, the breathing is abnormal. Other kinds of abnormal respiration include very slow or fast breathing, loud gasping, shallow breathing, or breathing with the mouth open. Adult and senior dogs at rest usually take 10 to 30 breaths a minute.

If your dog has a hard time breathing, or if you notice a nasal discharge, swelling, or foul odors coming from his nose, call your vet. These signs can signal the presence of a foreign object, tumor, or infection.

Capillary Refill Time (CRT)

CRT is the time it takes for the small blood vessels in the gums to refill with blood after you press them for a few

Age-Defying Tip

Give Them Space

Older dogs really appreciate their own space and bed, and you'll do your senior a huge favor by making sure that children and other dogs allow him to rest quietly when he wants to. He has earned some peace of mind.

seconds. A normal CRT is one to two seconds. A time of more than two seconds may indicate shock, dehydration, or heart failure.

Eyes

Although your senior's eyes may not shine as brightly as they did when he was young, they should still be healthy looking. Eye discharge is a warning sign that something is wrong, such as an eye infection. Infections can progress quickly and can even cause permanent eye damage.

As dogs grow older, they often develop iris atrophy, a condition in which the iris, which controls the amount of light that enters the eye, begins to shrink. As it does, too much light may strike the nerve fibers in the eyes, and the dog will squint to reduce the glare.

SENIOR TALES

"Mogo"

My friend Audrey relates, "I had an ancient Jack Russell Terrier, Mogo, who suddenly began walking around in circles. At first everyone assumed the dog had a vestibular problem that threw his balance off, or perhaps an ear infection. But no—the dog continued to walk in circles, hold his head to the side, and look miserable. Only after a sharp vet tech opened Mogo's mouth and carefully examined the back of his mouth did the culprit emerge: a very thin piece of wire that had somehow gotten wrapped around his back tooth and was obviously driving him nuts."

However, squinting also may signify other problems like a seed or other piece of debris irritating the eye. Even more serious, squinting can be an early sign of glaucoma. Eye problems can get worse quickly, so if you notice something that is not right, check with your vet.

Gums

Bad-looking gums can indicate problems with the teeth, circulation, breathing, infections, or even the liver. Normal gums are pink and healthy. Gums that are dark red could indicate infection; white gums signal anemia; yellow gums may point to liver problems; and dark blue gums suggest poor circulation. If your dog has dark-pigmented gums naturally, you can check for proper color by pulling down the skin just below the

Your senior's eyes may not shine as brightly as they did when he was young, but they still should be healthy looking

eye and examining the color of the inner eyelid—the eyelid will exhibit the same color changes as a "normal" pink gum. If you notice anything unusual, take your dog to the vet.

Heart Rate

A normal heart sound has two separate, drum-like, regular beats with a silent interval between them. You can place your hand on your dog's left side while he is lying down, or you can take his pulse along the femoral artery on the inner side of his upper leg. The normal heart rate for adult dogs, 70 to 180 beats per minute, doesn't change much with age. If your dog's heart rate isn't within the normal range, take him to the vet.

Nose

A dog nose is good for more than drawing in air—it's also an excellent smeller. No one knows how well dogs can really smell, but they may be able to detect odors in concentrations as small as ten parts per billion. Most dogs will experience some type of olfactory loss after the age of 14.

A healthy nose is usually a little moist due to mucus secretions. Nasal discharge, on the other hand, can be a sign of infectious disease, especially if accompanied by fever, lethargy, severe diarrhea or vomiting, or runny eyes. If you suspect a contagious disease, isolate your other dogs, and disinfect your hands and clothes before touching other dogs.

See your vet if these signs are present.

Temperature

The normal body temperature for a dog ranges from 99.5° to 102.5°F (37.5° to 39.2°C). Temperatures outside these ranges can indicate fever, hypothermia, hyperthermia, or other problems. Any temperature below 95°F (35°C) or over 106°F (41.1°C) is an emergency, and you must immediately take your senior to the vet.

To take your dog's temperature, buy a small digital thermometer and lubricate the tip with petroleum jelly. Ask someone to hold your dog while you insert the tip of the thermometer about 1 inch (2.5 cm) into the rectum. Remove it and read.

NEUTERING

Some people feel that if they adopt an older unneutered dog, it may be too late to have the animal neutered. This is not so. If the dog is healthy, he or she can be neutered at any age. Neutering older dogs is a responsible action that prevents them from contributing to the unwanted puppy problem and makes them more contented pets.

A neutered male's interest in roaming may be reduced by up to 90 percent. Also,

Most dogs will experience some type of olfactory loss after the age of 14.

Anesthesia in Older Dogs

If your vet suggests anesthesia to diagnose a problem, clean teeth, or do a similar noninvasive procedure, don't panic. While all anesthesia carries a slight risk, it's usually negligible. Older dogs can do very well under anesthesia, and if your dog has undergone anesthesia successfully before, there's no reason to think that he wouldn't do well again. Your vet will check his heart and do a panel to screen for any unusual problems, but fear of the dog dying under anesthesia is generally unfounded.

If your older dog is scheduled for surgery, your vet will certainly want to do some preanesthetic screening, which will evaluate liver and kidney function, blood components, and electrolytes. The results will tell your vet whether surgery should be postponed, whether a different type of anesthetic is advisable, or whether certain changes in the planned procedure need to be made. There are many different surgical options available today, such as laser surgery, that may be perfect for older dogs who may have a hard time with the anesthesia.

neutering your older male dog has beneficial effects on the prostate gland, which often becomes enlarged over the course of his life. An enlarged prostate is also liable to become infected. Once an older dog is neutered, however, the prostate gland shrinks noticeably. In addition, neutering older dogs helps to prevent certain kinds of hernias, as well as tumors of the testicles and even of the perianal area.

Spaying your female dog before her first heat cycle largely protects against mammary cancer. However, even older dogs can be safely spayed as long as they have strong hearts, and spaying a dog when she's a senior has benefits. For example, spaying a dog at any age removes the possibility of a severe infection of the uterus called pyometra. If you are going to have your older female spayed (or your older male castrated), your vet will want to perform some standard tests such as a routine blood count, serum biochemical tests, urinalysis, and perhaps a chest X-ray or EKG prior to anesthesia. You should be able to take your dog home in a day or so; your vet will prescribe some post-op drugs for pain. Stitches can be removed in approximately ten days.

MEDICATION

It's a fact that as they age, dogs may need to rely on medications to keep them healthy. If your vet prescribes a medication for your dog, don't leave the office without a clear understanding of what you're supposed to do with it. If there is something about the medication you don't understand, ask the vet. Here is the minimum of what you need to know about each medication your pet gets:

- what it is (you should know both the generic and trade names)
- what it's for
- what the correct dosage is
- when to give it and for how long
- how it should be administered
- what side effects it may have
- how it interacts with any other medications your senior is getting
- what improvement you should expect and in what time period

Purchasing Medication

When purchasing medication, you should know that, as with human medicines, some kinds are available in generic form. These are almost always cheaper and usually of the same quality as the "name brand." Although both products must meet minimum standards, sometimes the name brand does provide better ingredients. Ask your veterinarian about each drug that your senior needs.

Do not order medications and immunizations through the mail and administer them to your dog yourself, even if you know how to give shots. You may save some money, but in the long run, you'll be doing your dog a disservice. Here's why. When you take your dog to the vet, you are doing more than getting him a shot and going home; it's a chance to speak with her about your concerns and observations. It's important for the veterinarian to see your dog when he's healthy as well as when he's sick. A good veterinarian will always give your dog a checkup at the same time. More selfishly, I always feel that going to my regular vet for routine care gives me the right to call him up at home at midnight (which I have done) during an emergency.

How to Give Medication

Dispensing medication correctly assures that you are giving the right medication at the right time

Squirt liquid medications in the "pouch" between the teeth and cheek.

in the right dosage. The obvious first step is to follow your vet's instructions to the letter—the directions on the package also may help.

Pills

If you are a no-nonsense person, the easiest and quickest way to give a dog a pill is to open his mouth and stick the pill far enough back in the throat that he can't spit it out. This usually works quite well. But if your dog really resists, you have to resort to trickery, such as hiding the pill in a bit of peanut butter, cheese, marshmallow, bread, or frankfurter. Or stick it in his food soaked in broth. There are also new edible "pill pockets," tasty little pita bread-like treats that are designed to hold a pill.

If you don't have a handy treat in which to hide the pill, simply hold your dog's upper jaw between your thumb and index finger. Tilt the head back, folding his upper lip over the front teeth (to protect you). Then pop the pill far back into the mouth, and immediately shut it.

Squirt liquid medications in the "pouch" between the teeth and cheek.

Eye Medication

To administer eye medication, stand behind your dog and place one hand on the side of his head to hold the head still and open the eye. Then apply the medication with the other hand. Apply the required amount directly into the eye.

Ear Medication

Most dogs who are given ear medications have an ear infection—and they do not like their ears being touched. Drape one arm over the animal, if necessary holding his legs close to the elbows to prevent him from getting up and leaving. With your other hand, squeeze the directed amount of medicine into the ear. Follow the label instructions, which may direct you to massage the ear afterward.

VACCINATING YOUR SENIOR DOG

One of the greatest controversies in the dog world is the vaccination fracas. Questions arise about which dogs should be vaccinated for what disease, how often, and at what age to stop. While nobody questions the importance of vaccines for youngsters, their efficacy, safety, and even need is a real hot-button issue when it comes to seniors. The trend is for less frequent vaccination. However, some research indicates that the immune systems of older dogs are not as effective as those of younger dogs, and some people believe that seniors may benefit from more frequent vaccinations than their younger counterparts. Other veterinarians belong to the "if-the-dog-isn't-immune-by-now-he-never-will-be" school of thought. The best plan is to talk over your options with your veterinarian.

How Vaccines Work

A vaccine works by exercising the body's immune system. It increases both the number of cells "trained" to destroy a particular pathogen and also the speed at which the immune system can respond to a threat. A vaccine contains just a tiny bit of the offending substance in a dose of fluid that is injected into the animal. Some vaccines are called "killed" vaccines because the pathogen is indeed completely inert. In other vaccines, the pathogen is "attenuated"; that means that it's still alive but very weak. Newer vaccines sometimes use only pieces of the original pathogen—enough to make the immune system think that it's dealing with the real thing but not enough to do it any harm. The immune system is very smart, but it gets fooled into thinking that the vaccine is the real deal and behaves accordingly, conferring immunity upon the body just as if it had fought off a real case of distemper or rabies, for example.

Most vaccinations are given in early puppyhood, but they last for years. This means that your senior dog, if he has been vaccinated as a young adult, may retain some of his immunity to the disease for which he was vaccinated. Exceptions are bordetella vaccines, which, like many vaccines against bacterial infections, are good for only six months or so.

If you adopt a senior dog and do not know his vaccination history, your vet may recommend that he be completely vaccinated all over again. This is a wise precaution.

Vaccination Risks

Vaccines save millions of human and animal lives every year. Along with anesthesia and antibiotics, they are among the greatest contributions to medicine. However, they are not always entirely

SENIOR TALES

"Tulip"

Sometimes what can save your dog's life will save yours as well. My friend Cindy had been a two-pack-a-day smoker for 20 years. Nothing could induce her to quit—until the day she took her dog to the vet for a routine checkup. Tulip had been suffering from some itchy skin problems. After some tough questioning, Cindy and the vet determined that Tulip might be suffering an allergic reaction to cigarette smoke. (The more time the dog spent inside Cindy's smoke-filled apartment, the more itchy she seemed to be.) Cindy also learned that dogs who inhale secondhand smoke are three times more likely to develop lung or nasal cancer than dogs who live in a smoke-free environment. The alarmed Cindy managed to give up her habit. "I did it for the dog," she told me frankly.

Seniors who frequently meet other dogs should be vaccinated against communicable diseases.

without risk. Some animals have adverse reactions to them, and the immunity that vaccines grant against dangerous diseases is not always complete. Some veterinarians believe that vaccinations can weaken the immune system and ultimately increase an animal's propensity to developing allergies, cancers, epilepsy, and hypothyroidism. Evidence for this is shaky, but it's not impossible. However, returning to the days before vaccines is unthinkable.

Modern dog owners can have the best of both worlds by vaccinating their dogs responsibly against common diseases. It is safer to avoid some of the "multiple" vaccines, which, though convenient, may stress your dog's system. Annual boosters of most anti-viral vaccines are neither desirable nor necessary.

In rare cases, your senior dog might react negatively to a vaccine. However, compared with the risks of *not* vaccinating, those risks are tiny. The most severe and rarest (one in every 15,000 vaccinations) reaction is anaphylaxis, a life-threatening, immediate allergic reaction to something injected. Anaphylactic reactions are more commonly associated with the use of killed vaccines like rabies, canine coronavirus, and leptospirosis. That's because killed vaccines have more viral or bacterial particles per dose and also have added chemicals to boost the dog's immune response. These same features increase the risk of an allergic response.

If untreated, anaphylaxis results in shock, respiratory distress, and cardiac failure. This reaction usually occurs within minutes to less than 24 hours after the vaccination. If you think that your dog is having an anaphylactic reaction, seek emergency veterinary care right away.

Vaccinating Against Common Diseases

The diseases against which your dog needs to be vaccinated depend upon several factors:

- **Lifestyle.** Seniors who frequently meet other dogs or who are boarded are most at risk for communicable diseases. Boarding kennels also require certain vaccines. On the other hand, a single stay-at-home senior is less at risk.

- **Location.** Certain diseases are more common in some areas than in others. It is not necessary for your dog to get vaccinated against a disease that doesn't occur where you live.

- **Your vet's protocol.** Different vets have different theories about what vaccine senior dogs should have and how often. Some believe that senior dogs are about as immune as they are going to be, and further vaccination does no good. Others contend that the senior immune system is weaker and needs boosting. Talk with your vet about her protocol.

The following are some diseases against which seniors are often vaccinated.

Bordetella (Kennel Cough)

This is a highly contagious airborne disease characterized by coughing. If your dog boards or kennels a lot or mingles with other dogs, this vaccine is important. It needs to be given about every six months to be effective.

Canine Adenovirus

This is a cause of hepatitis in dogs and can result in severe liver damage and respiratory infection.

> **⊰ Senior Moment ⊱**
>
> **Cleanliness**
>
> Cleanliness is next to dogliness. Older dogs greatly benefit from frequent, careful grooming and bathing, as well as washing of their bedding. Dirty fur and bedding lead to insect infestations, sores, and discomfort.

Vaccines save millions of lives every year.

Canine Distemper

Related to human measles, distemper is a highly contagious and often fatal viral disease that can be transmitted through all bodily secretions. It also can become airborne. It attacks the respiratory, gastrointestinal, and nervous systems. Signs include eye and nasal discharge, fever, coughing, loss of appetite, vomiting, diarrhea, twitching, and paralysis. Even dogs who live through it are often permanently affected.

Canine Parvovirus

A contagious disease that spreads by oral contamination of infected feces. It attacks the intestines, immune system, and heart muscle. While most dangerous to puppies, it's no picnic for any dog. Parvo is characterized by smelly diarrhea that is often bloody, vomiting, dehydration, and in severe cases, fever and lowered white blood cell count. Death can occur as early as two days after the onset of the disease. Vaccinations have helped to control the spread of this disease, but despite being vaccinated, some dogs still contract parvovirus and often die from it.

Rabies

This fatal disease is caused by a bullet-shaped virus and is transmitted by contact with the saliva of an infected animal, usually through a bite. Any mammal can contract rabies, although raccoons, skunks, foxes, bats, and occasionally groundhogs are the most common victims. The incubation period can last from several weeks to a year or more. Once an animal is infected, the virus travels along the nerves to the spinal cord and then to the brain. You can never be absolutely certain that a dog has contracted rabies just by observation because the signs of rabies are extremely variable (the disease has several stages, with different symptoms for each stage), often mimicking those of other diseases. Some dogs become aggressive, others confused and disoriented. There is no known cure, and if not treated before symptoms develop, the disease is fatal.

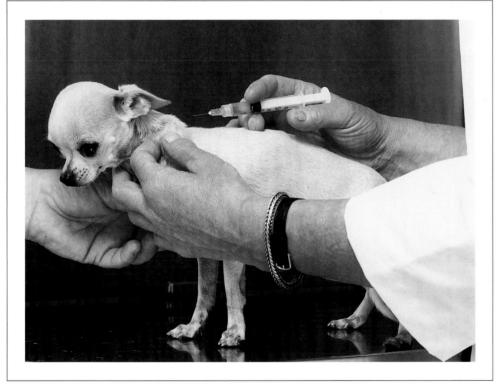

If you adopt a senior dog and do not know his vaccination history, your vet may recommend that he be completely vaccinated again.

Pain in Dogs

Dogs are notably stoic about pain. In the wild, a sick or injured animal is in danger of being attacked by his rivals, so it is possible that dogs developed the strategy of pretending nothing was wrong for as long as possible. The truth is that by the time you notice your animal is in pain, he may have been trying to hide it for days.

Dogs in pain tend to become very quiet, move around less, and show reluctance to engage in walks or stair climbing. They often lose their appetite and may shiver or pant. Any unusual behavior on the part of your dog should signal to you that there is something wrong.

You can test for pain by gently running your hands over your dog's body, including the paws. An unusual reaction further suggests there's a problem, and it's time for a trip to the vet. Never give human medications to your dog in an attempt to make him more comfortable without conferring with your vet. Some human pain relievers, like Tylenol, are quite dangerous to dogs.

PARASITES

Parasites can take a toll on older dogs because they have fewer resources and reserves of strength to fight them off. Be especially vigilant in keeping them off and out of your dog.

External Parasites

External parasites, as the name suggests, are those that live on your dog. The most common ones are fleas, mites, and ticks.

Fleas

Your older dog needs and deserves a flea-free existence. When these parasites bite, they inject saliva under the dog's skin to prevent blood coagulation. Many dogs are allergic to the saliva, and a single fleabite can cause severe itching or even hives. Some dogs chew themselves until they are hairless. Fleas also carry tapeworm and other diseases.

To destroy the enemy, it helps to understand the four-stage life cycle of the flea, which can complete itself in about a month:

- **Eggs:** Females may lay several hundred eggs at once, either on your dog, in the rug, or in the yard. They are smooth and slick, so eggs laid directly on the dog fall off on the carpet or grass.

- **Larvae:** The blind larvae hatch from the eggs and live on dried blood, dander, and other organic stuff lying around. Larvae do not suck blood, but they do spin cocoons.

- **Pupae:** The pupae are the cocooned fleas. They usually remain cocooned for 3 to 14 days but can remain dormant for much longer if necessary.
- **Adult:** Adult fleas jump onto the dog.

The good news is that fleas can be controlled, especially with the newer oral and systemic "spot-on" treatments. For best results, treat all pets and their quarters at the same time. Your vacuum cleaner is your best friend here! As soon as you vacuum, throw the bag out—otherwise you are providing the perfect incubator for these invaders.

Preventing fleas is obviously the easiest way to control them, and you have plenty of choices. Insect growth regulators (IGRs) control fleas by interrupting their development.

Adulticides kill the flea outright. Spot-on products are liquids applied onto your pet's skin between the shoulders at monthly intervals. The medication is absorbed into your pet's skin and distributed throughout his body through the sebaceous glands, interfering with the fleas' nervous system while not adversely affecting the dog. Talk

Check your dog for fleas and ticks after he's been playing outside.

Common External Parasites

Common external parasites include fleas, mites, and ticks.

with your vet about the best flea prevention and/or treatment plan for your dog.

Mites

Mites are tiny arachnids that cause mange. In seniors, the most common type of mite is the sarcoptic mange mite, or scabies mite, which burrows into the upper layer of the skin. This mite is highly contagious and causes a tremendous amount of itching and scabbiness, especially around the face, ears, and elbows.

Only a vet can diagnose this condition. She will likely prescribe a miticide and recommend that you treat all other dogs in your household.

Ticks

The life cycle of the tick is somewhat similar to that of fleas. The female tick can lay 100 to 6,000 eggs, depending on the species. Tick larvae have six legs until they have their first blood meal, at which time they molt into eight-legged nymphs. The nymphs then molt into adult ticks and can live from a few months to several years.

If your dog acquires a tick, don a pair of gloves, use a tissue, or employ a handy commercial tick removal tool. Grasp the tick as close to the head as possible and pull it straight out without squeezing. Then toss it into the toilet and flush. Many times the area where the tick has attached itself will become red and angry looking; however, that is not because the head of the tick was left in. It's simply a reaction. Keep the area dry and clean, and it will heal. If the tick's head is still embedded in your dog, take him to the vet.

Ticks can be controlled by some of the same products that kill fleas. Talk with your vet for more information.

Internal Parasites

There are many types of internal parasites that can infect a dog. In fact, older dogs can get a variety of these parasites, including heartworms, hookworms, tapeworms, and whipworms.

Heartworms

Heartworm disease is spread by mosquitoes in whose digestive tract the microfilariae (baby heartworms) mature. After two molts, the third larval stage develops into an infective agent. While tiny when they enter the system, the worms grow to be 1 foot (0.3 m) long! After about five months in the body, they enter the large vessels of the lungs and heart.

Heartworms cause fatigue, coughing, and heart disease, but signs of heartworm disease may not be apparent for several years after initial infection. Untreated, the condition is always fatal. A good heartworm preventive can prevent not only heartworms but also roundworms, whipworms, and hookworms. Dogs who live in areas affected by heartworms (which is most of the US) should be kept on a preventive year-round.

Treatment for heartworm disease involves first destroying the adult worms and then eliminating the microfilariae. Risks of therapy are directly related to the number of heartworms and the degree of lung involvement, which increases the incidence of clots in the lungs. According to the American Heartworm Society, senior dogs who have an advanced case of heartworm disease may have damaged internal organs that could make treatment difficult. However, if the dog is otherwise healthy and is prevented from overexercising, the prognosis is good.

Hookworms

Hookworms are small, thin worms that attach to the lining of the intestinal wall; they feed on a dog's blood and can cause blood loss. When the worm lays its eggs, they pass through the feces into the environment, where the larvae hatch and live in the soil. Your dog can contract hookworm by ingesting the larvae or even by stepping on them—they can penetrate the skin. While hooks are more serious in puppies (who in serious cases may even need a transfusion), older dogs can develop chronic diarrhea and lose weight. Your vet can examine your dog's feces for evidence of the worms. The most effective way to keep your dog from getting hookworms is to make sure that he is on a monthly heartworm medication that also prevents hookworms.

Tapeworms

Although hideous in almost every way, tapeworms do not usually pose a serious threat to your senior dog's health. But who wants them? Most dogs who spend a lot of time outdoors may end up with them—either from swallowing an infected flea or eating a dead animal. Tapeworms live out their lives in your dog's intestinal tract; their presence is betrayed by the rice-like body segments that emerge with his stools. The most frequent sign of tapeworm infestation is itching, although a few dogs develop fatigue or fever.

Your vet can give your dog medication to get rid of tapeworms.

Whipworms

This small but nasty worm takes up residence in the dog's cecum (part of the bowel), sucking blood and laying eggs that pass with the dog's stool. A large number of whipworms can

Common Internal Parasites

Common internal parasites include heartworms, hookworms, tapeworms, and whipworms.

produce chronic and dangerous diarrhea and blood loss. Worming the dog removes all trace of these signs.

Whipworm eggs can be hard to find in a fecal sample because female whipworms don't lay their eggs constantly, so they can be missed. There is a variety of different substances that control whipworms. Many monthly heartworm medications also control whipworms.

DIET

A good diet is essential to your senior's wellness. Older dogs who are less active need fewer calories; however, because they don't absorb nutrients as well as younger dogs do, the foods they do eat need to be extremely nourishing and of high quality. The golden years are no time to fill up on junk food. Your job is to supply a healthy diet with top-notch ingredients that give your dog's body what it needs.

Some older dogs become progressively more picky as they age, possibly because their senses of smell and taste are failing; others seem to want to eat anything. Both of these conditions could be normal, but both also could be a sign of a disease condition. If your dog's eating habits change, talk to your veterinarian.

Obesity is a major problem in dogs but is also completely preventable. Keep close tabs on your dog's weight, and not only because a trim dog is a healthy dog. Unexplained weight gain or weight loss may be the first sign of disease.

A good diet is essential to your senior's wellness.

Physical exercise is critically important for older dogs—it helps to control weight, maintain muscle mass, improve mobility, and aid circulation.

If you need to change your dog's diet, do so gradually, because the digestive systems of older dogs respond poorly to sudden changes. Increase the amount of new food gradually over a period of about a week or so.

See Chapter 3 for complete details on feeding the senior dog.

EXERCISE: PHYSICAL AND MENTAL

Just because your dog is getting on in years does not mean that he should be relegated to the couch. Physical exercise is critically important for older dogs. It helps to control weight, maintain muscle mass, improve mobility, and aid circulation. To keep your senior safe when exercising, modify his activities to avoid leaping and twisting, and avoid high-endurance sports. Older dogs don't need to jump through hoops to get exercise. A gentle walk will often do the trick, and just petting and talking to your dog

Your senior dog needs mental exercise to stay healthy and alert.

does much for the canine soul. The most important thing to remember is to know and respect your dog's limits.

Mental exercise is important too. Try playing a game of hide-and-seek, or engage in quick training sessions. Even going on a slow walk is mental stimulus for a dog, who will find every passing shrub infinitely interesting.

See Chapter 6 for details on how to exercise with your senior dog.

EMERGENCIES

An emergency is a serious and unexpected health crisis. Fortunately, you can improve the chances of a happy outcome to any emergency by preparing for it. Keep in mind that older dogs have less resilience than younger ones do, so don't rely on "natural healing"; you need to work fast, safely, and efficiently, and you must immediately take your dog to the nearest vet.

Bleeding

Gently apply pressure to the area with a clean cloth. Don't remove the cloth—just transport your dog to the vet. If your pet is vomiting blood, has blood in the stool, or is coughing up blood, take him to the vet immediately.

Choking

If your dog is choking, gently attempt to look in his mouth to remove obstructions. If none are visible, perform the Heimlich maneuver. To do this, place your fist just behind the ribs and compress the abdomen three to five times in quick thrusts. If the object is not expelled, take your dog to the vet immediately.

Disasters

None of us can know when a disaster may strike. Hurricanes, floods, or even a nuclear disaster can happen, even if we don't want to think about it. However, by being prepared and having a plan, the chances are that you, your family, and your senior dog will survive and even prosper. The time to prepare for a disaster is before it strikes. Here's what to do:

- Assemble a first-aid kit and an animal evacuation kit.
- Keep an emergency supply of food and water on hand.
- ID your dog with a visible ID and rabies tag. Tattoos and microchips are also excellent but should not be used in place of visible ID. Put ID tags on all carriers as well.
- Check all pet transport cages to make sure that they are in good condition. The following information should be clearly and indelibly printed on each one: your name; telephone numbers; address; a description of your pet (species, breed, sex, identifying marks, name); your vet's contact info; rabies tag number; microchip ID or tattoo ID; pet insurance policy number; and contact information for another person in case you are not home.

Reacting to an Emergency

Preparation is key to ensuring a successful outcome to an emergency. Have a first-aid kit on hand, as well as your emergency contact information.

First-Aid Kit

You can never tell when disaster will strike on a personal level—with your dog. Your dog's first-aid kit should be ready at hand and should contain the following:

- antidiarrhea medications
- bandages (gauze rolls, tape, nonstick pads)
- Benadryl for allergic reactions or carsickness
- cold/heat packs
- compact thermal blanket
- cortisone spray or cream
- cotton balls or wipes
- disinfectant
- disposable gloves
- ear cleaning solution
- emergency contact numbers: your regular vet, a 24-hour emergency clinic (and directions), and poison control center numbers
- eyedropper
- eyewash solution or lubricant
- first-aid booklet
- hydrogen peroxide (to make dog vomit)
- lubricant (petroleum jelly)
- magnifying glass
- muzzle (even good dogs bite when hurt or frightened—however, don't muzzle a dog who is unconscious or who is bleeding from the mouth)
- nail clippers
- needle-nose pliers or hemostat
- penlight
- plastic syringe to administer liquid medications
- rehydrating solution (Gatorade, Pedialyte)
- saline solution (sterile)
- scissors
- short nylon leash
- stethoscope
- styptic powder
- thermometer
- topical antibiotic
- towels (paper and cloth)
- tweezers

The time to prepare for a disaster is before it strikes.

- Place stickers on your windows and door in case of a fire, indicating to fire personnel what animals are in the home. Keep this up to date (and date it). If you have two dogs and one passes away, you don't want the firefighters risking their lives looking for your second dog! You also may list where the dog is likely to be found.

- Keep proof of ownership with you in your wallet or purse, along with a clear picture of your dog and you together.

- Learn the evacuation plan for your city.

- Keep a list of contact people who can care for your dog if you get separated. One copy should be by your phone, one attached to the crate, and one in your wallet. You can even purchase a tiny attachment to your dog's collar that contains some of this information—at least one telephone number besides your own.

- Make a list of kennels and dog-accepting hotels within a 100-mile (160.9-km) radius of your home.

Dog Bites

If your dog is bitten by another dog, clean the wound gently with lukewarm water, and disinfect it with a wound cleaner. If it looks serious, call a vet.

Frostbite

Frostbite occurs when a dog is exposed to freezing temperatures, and older dogs with diabetes or who are on beta blockers are at increased risk for frostbite. Because the body struggles to keep its core warm, external parts such as the ears and toes are usually affected first and most seriously. Affected skin may appear reddened or gray. If your dog has frostbite, apply warm cloths to the area, or place the affected feet in a bowl of warm water. Do not apply direct heat, like that from a hair dryer. Dry the area carefully—do not massage it or you could further damage the tissue. Then, take your senior to the vet.

Heatstroke

Exercising in the heat, being locked up in a warm car, dehydration, obesity, and age are all factors that make dogs susceptible to heatstroke. In fact, older dogs produce fewer of the hormones needed to maintain the body's normal temperature. As the body's temperature rises, cells in the brain, intestine, and liver start to break down. Blood thickens and stagnates. Tissue dies—and so can your dog.

The older and larger your dog is, the greater a candidate he is for heatstroke. (Short-snouted dogs are also more at risk.) For instance, small-breed dogs are at greatest risk at the age of 14 and older, but large-breed dogs become increasingly vulnerable by only 7 years of age. Old dogs are also more likely to have cardiovascular problems, so their less efficient circulatory system makes overheating even more dangerous for them. (A poor circulatory system does not circulate blood efficiently through the skin, where most of the cooling takes place.)

If you suspect heatstroke, take your dog's temperature. A rectal temperature of 105°F (40.6°C) or above is indicative of heatstroke. And the longer the temperature stays there, the more dangerous it gets. Other signs include:

- bright red tongue and gums
- pale gums

Senior Dogs and Heatstroke

Senior dogs are more susceptible to heatstroke because their bodies produce fewer of the hormones needed to maintain the body's normal temperature.

The older and larger your dog is, the greater a candidate he is for heatstroke.

- panting
- salivating or vomiting
- sluggishness
- staggering and disorientation
- weakness
- wide open, staring eyes

Heatstroke is a life-threatening emergency, so get your dog in a cool place as fast as you can. Run cool water over him with a hose, or place him in a tub under cool running water. Make sure that the water actually touches the skin—not just the coat. Soak the belly, paw pads, and inside the legs. Run the water over the tongue. Don't put ice on the dog; that can cause skin injury and constrict the veins, locking the heat inside.

The smaller the dog, the faster he will cool down. Take his rectal temperature periodically, and stop cooling him down when it reaches 104° or 103°F (40° or 39.4°C). Don't try to cool him down any further because the cooling process will continue for a while.

Get your dog to your vet as soon as you can, where he may receive oxygen, cortisone, and dextrose to protect his body's damaged cells. IV fluids also may be administered.

Poisoning

If you think that your dog has been poisoned or received too much of a prescribed medication, contact your vet or one of the animal poison hotlines (listed below):

- **ASPCA National Animal Poison Control Center:** (900) 443-0000. (There is a charge per case, which is billed directly to the caller's phone.)

- **1-888-4ANI-HELP:** (888) 426-4435. (There is a charge per case, which is billed to the caller's credit card. Follow-up calls can be made for no additional charge by dialing (888) 299-2973.)

- **Animal Poison Hotline:** (888) 232-8870. (There is a charge per case, which is billed to the caller's credit card.)

Seizures

If your dog is seizing, protect him by clearing a space around him. Your dog is not aware of his surroundings, so do not touch his face or he may bite reflexively. Speak quietly to your dog and time the seizure. If it is not over in two minutes or so, take him to the vet.

Shock

Shock is a life-threatening condition in which the circulatory system collapses and the body's cells do not receive sufficient oxygen. It is usually caused by loss of blood and can occur as a result of trauma. Even sunstroke, which damages the blood vessels, can induce shock, as can pneumonia or lung damage—both common in older animals.

Signs of shock include rapid heart rate, because the heart is working harder and harder to pump the blood. A simple test for shock is capillary refill time. All you need to do is press on the gum for a second and then remove your finger. If the pink color does not return in a second or two, your dog may be going into shock. Immediately get him to the vet for emergency care—he needs fluids and oxygen immediately.

❧ Senior Moment ❧

Canine CPR

It never hurts to learn canine CPR for emergencies. Your local chapter of the American Red Cross may offer training. Go to www.redcross.org/services/hss/courses/pfachapter.html to find out.

Alternative therapies can be valuable adjuncts to regular veterinary care for senior dogs.

ALTERNATIVE THERAPIES

In addition to standard veterinary care, many people seek out alternative care such as acupuncture, chiropractic, herbal medicine, homeopathy, and massage therapy. Some of these therapies can be valuable adjuncts to regular veterinary care for seniors as well as younger dogs. In any case, talk with your veterinarian before embarking upon them.

Acupuncture

Acupuncture has been practiced for more than 3,000 years. It is a therapy based on ancient Chinese medicine in which the nerve endings (called "meridians" in traditional Chinese medicine) are stimulated by small-gauge needles.

The exact way in which acupuncture works is not well understood, but it has claimed some remarkable successes, especially for seniors with arthritis, nerve damage, cardiovascular disorders, and urinary incontinence. For some reason, animals do not seem to mind the insertion of the needles. It may take four to eight sessions to achieve the desired outcome. For best results, seek a veterinary acupuncturist who is a member of the American Academy of Veterinary Acupuncture (AAVA).

Chiropractic

Unlike acupuncture, veterinary chiropractic is a fairly new modality in veterinary medicine. Chiropractors work on "adjusting" certain biomechanical problems that arise that may cause pain or interfere with correct movement. To do this, joints are manipulated in a series of thrusts. Proponents claim that it works to treat not only "obvious" problems like joint and muscle pain common in senior dogs, but also dogs with hypothyroidism, liver disorders, digestive problems, mitral valve insufficiencies in older dogs, anxiety, and lick granulomas. No independent research backs up claims for any of the latter problems, though.

For best results, choose a vet who is a member of the American Veterinary Chiropractic Association (AVCA).

Herbal Medicine

Many medications, even standard medicine, derive from herbs. Aspirin, for instance, comes from willow trees. However, when herbal medicine (either Western herbal or Chinese herbal) is used as a modality, the herbs are used in their whole state, not reduced to their chemical constituents. Proponents believe that herbal remedies work more gently than the medicines derived from them and are thus extremely well suited to senior dogs, whose aging systems need a kinder touch. Herbs can be used to treat a variety of diseases, from arthritis to cancer. For best results, seek a practitioner who is a member of the Veterinary Botanical Medical Association (VBMA).

Homeopathy

Developed in the 1700s, homeopathy uses minute amounts of substances that can cause the symptoms of the disease if given in larger amounts. For example, if a dog has hives, the typical homeopathic remedy is "apis," a substance derived from a whole ground-up bee. The theory ("like cures like") is that because bees sting and can induce hives, the remedy is to give the patient a tiny amount of bee that has been sufficiently shaken up to "energize" it.

Ask the Vet

Talk with your veterinarian before deciding on an alternative therapy for your senior.

While homeopathy is largely harmless, some homeopathic practitioners do not allow their patients to be treated with regular medicines at the same time, and that can be dangerous. No peer-reviewed scientific studies have ever shown homeopathy to be an effective treatment. Consider choosing a practitioner who is a member of the Academy of Veterinary Homeopathy (AVH).

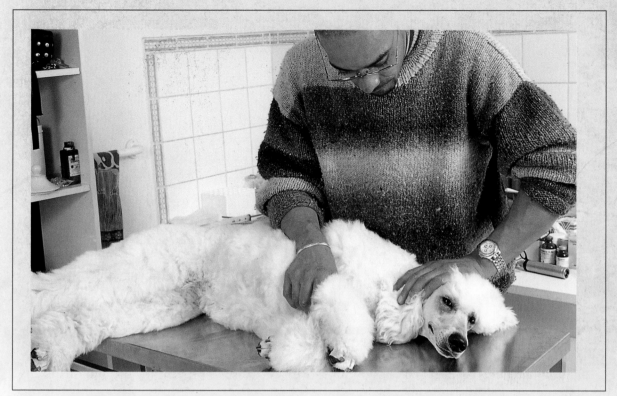

Canine massage can ease muscle stiffness and help your senior relax.

Massage Therapy

A good massage does wonders for the mind and body—especially the aging mind and body. It is excellent for easing muscle stiffness and helping a dog relax. Massage therapy covers everything from simple stretching and range-of-motion activities to more invasive treatments. While there are professional canine massage therapists, you can learn many simple techniques yourself and use them to your dog's advantage.

Your older dog deserves the best care, and we are lucky to live in a time when so many options for great care exist, from ancient Chinese medicine to state-of-the-art MRIs. There's never been a better time to be a senior dog or a senior dog owner!

Chapter 8

DISORDERS AND DISEASES OF SENIOR DOGS

While dogs of any age can fall prey to disease, the facts of life are that older dogs are at greater risk for all kinds of disease conditions. Their joints are stiffer, muscles weaker, and teeth less perfect than those of young adults. Their internal organs are less efficient, and they have more trouble regulating their temperature.

Older dogs also have fewer resources to fight infections and other diseases common to all dogs. The good news is that with excellent preventive care, good nutrition, and plenty of love, your dog can prosper well into old age. This chapter provides a comprehensive list of many senior ailments, along with signs to help you figure out what's wrong and possible treatments your vet may administer.

CANCER

Cancer is an extremely common ailment of old dogs. In fact, it accounts for about half of the deaths of dogs over ten years of age. To make things worse, the word "cancer" often brings such an emotional response in people that they react with terror and feel paralyzed, unable to take action. And it is true that cancer is a major killer of senior dogs. But this doesn't mean that all cases are hopeless or that there is nothing you can do.

Cancer is defined as a malignant cellular tumor and results when the body fails to recognize and destroy cells that do not replicate normally. A cancer may be localized, or

Your older dog can prosper well into old age if given excellent preventive care, good nutrition, and lots of love.

it may invade adjacent tissues and spread through the body. Some tumors are benign, meaning that they don't spread. A malignant tumor, on the other hand, spreads (metastasizes) and invades healthy tissue; this can occur in any location or body system.

General Signs

General signs of cancer include:

- a sore that does not heal
- an unexplained lump, especially one increasing in size
- appetite loss or eating problem
- breathing difficulty
- change in bladder or bowel patterns
- foul odor of the breath or body
- lameness or stiffness
- unexplained bleeding or discharge
- weight loss

Prevention

Most of the time, the cause of cancer is unknown and so is not possible to prevent. However, there is one important exception: mammary cancer. If you have your female dog spayed before her first heat cycle, her chances of coming down with this cancer in old age are much reduced. If you have an unspayed older dog, follow the advice of your veterinarian about getting her spayed.

General Treatment

In a nutshell, there are three basic methods of treating cancer: surgery (with a scalpel),

Chemotherapy treats cancer with powerful drugs that course through the body.

chemotherapy (with drugs), and radiation (usually with X-rays). Often a combination of these methods is used. If your dog develops cancer, talk with your vet about your options. While most people understand in general how cancer surgery works, they may be unsure about radiation and chemotherapy and the differences between them.

In some cases, treatment is meant to be curative, meaning that the cancer is eliminated and the dog is cured. This can cause a lot of side effects, however, and it may not be effective. Often, veterinarians and dog owners choose "palliative care," which uses lower doses and has fewer side effects. This approach does not kill the cancer but can extend the life of the dog and make him comfortable by getting rid of many symptoms like pain and bleeding.

Surgery

The purpose of surgery is to remove or repair damaged tissues. With modern anesthesia and pain-killing drugs, surgery is both effective and comparatively pain free. Some cancers, if localized and caught early, can be completely cured with surgery. For others, surgery can buy weeks or months of time.

Chemotherapy

Chemotherapy involves treating cancer with powerful drugs. With this treatment method, drugs are given either orally or intravenously. They go through the entire body, even places where there is no cancer. Side effects include fatigue and sometimes stomach upset, but they are not nearly as pronounced as they are in human beings.

Radiation

Radiation is a local treatment aimed right at the tumor. It works by knocking atoms apart that attack the cells—it has a greater effect on growing cells (like the ones in tumors) than in nongrowing ones. It also can reach areas that may be unreachable by a scalpel. Researchers expect to see image-guided radiation therapy very soon, which will make this treatment method even more "on target."

Common Cancers in Senior Dogs

Certain cancers are more common in senior dogs, including bone cancer, lymphoma, mast cell tumors, and transitional cell carcinoma.

Bone Cancer

Bone cancer is most common in large dogs, although it can appear in any breed. Old dogs are the most likely victims. Four kinds of bone cancer can occur, with the most common being osteosarcoma, accounting for about 80 percent of bone cancers.

Osteosarcoma arises from cells that produce bone. It is the most dangerous of the bone cancers and is most often seen in the long bones of big breeds, like Saint Bernards, Great Danes, and Mastiffs. Other affected breeds include Irish Setters, Doberman Pinchers, German Shepherd Dogs, and Golden Retrievers. Other forms include chondrosarcomas (arising from the cartilage joint surfaces), fibrosarcomas (originating from fibrous connective tissue), and synovial cell carcinomas (originating from joint tissues).

The first line of treatment for bone cancer is often amputation; fortunately, most dogs tolerate amputation well and adapt easily to a three-legged life.

The Cancer Diet

The correct diet is critical if your dog has cancer. He will need high-quality (meat-based) protein and fatty acids. Two things he does not need are grains and carbohydrates. Tumors thrive on carbohydrates while robbing the body of amino acids, but they can't metabolize fat. The bottom line? Feed a diet with increased fat content and good-quality protein to slow tumor growth, and a minimum amount of carbohydrates—the fewer the better.

SIGNS

Signs of bone cancer include sudden lameness with a gradually increasing swelling near a joint. X-rays often will reveal changes in the bone that don't look anything like the kind arthritis causes.

TREATMENT

If the cancer has not spread, the first line of treatment is amputation, or removal of the affected limb. If accompanied by chemotherapy, treatment can be successful. The exact kind of chemotherapy used depends on the overall health of the dog as well as how well his heart and kidneys are functioning. Most dogs tolerate amputation extremely well and adapt easily to a three-legged life.

Lymphoma

This is a common cancer of the lymphatic system. It occurs in many breeds, particularly Boxers, Basset Hounds, Saint Bernards, Pointers, Airedale Terriers, Bulldogs, and certain lines of Bullmastiffs, Otterhounds, Rottweilers, and Scottish Terriers.

SIGNS

Signs of lymphoma are extremely variable, often depending on where the cancer is located. Many dogs do not seem sick at all. Others become tired and have decreased appetite and weight loss, vomiting, diarrhea, and swelling of the lymph nodes.

TREATMENT

Intravenous chemotherapy is the treatment of choice. It is rarely curative but can produce a remission lasting for many months.

Mast Cell Tumors

The most common malignant skin cancer in dogs is mast cell tumors. Affected dogs are, on average, about eight years old. Mast cells are normal cells in the body that are important components of the immune system. They contain substances (histamines) that are released when an allergic reaction occurs and cause the familiar signs of an allergy. The most common sites for mast cell tumors are the skin of the trunk and perineal region and the skin of the extremities. Schnauzers, Beagles, Labrador Retrievers, and Boston Terriers are most disposed to this kind of tumor.

SIGNS

Mast cell tumors present a variety of signs depending on the system affected and the "grade" of the tumor. Often there is a skin tumor that may fluctuate in size.

TREATMENT

Your vet may want to take a biopsy to recommend a course of action. If the mast cell tumor does not confine itself to the skin and spreads to other organs, surgery may not be possible. This could be true even if the mast cell tumor is not particularly malignant. If surgery is not possible, radiation therapy or chemotherapy may be options. Radiation therapy is extremely effective for controlling a localized tumor. Chemotherapy medications can induce a remission in almost a quarter of the tumors.

Transitional Cell Carcinoma

Transitional cell carcinoma is a tumor of the bladder; the bladder tumor also can invade the prostate. Most affected dogs are elderly females averaging 11 years of age. Shetland Sheepdogs and Scottish Terriers seem highly predisposed. The cause of the disease is largely unknown, although we do know that certain chemotherapy drugs can induce it.

SIGNS

Signs of transitional cell carcinoma include bloody urine and straining to urinate, although these signs are also typical of other conditions such as severe bladder infection or a bladder stone. Your vet will diagnose the disease with a urinalysis and culture. X-rays are the next step, perhaps followed by a bladder tumor antigen test, which is an immunological analysis that detects antibodies produced in response to bladder tumor antigens (foreign substances in the body that evoke an immune response). Special imaging like ultrasound or cystoscopy also may be required.

TREATMENT

Unfortunately, there is no good surgical option for this cancer unless it is very small at the time of removal. A radical surgical option is ureterocolonic anastomosis—

⮜ Senior Moment ⮞

Chief Causes of Death in Seniors

The chief causes of death in older dogs, in order of most common to least common, are: (1) heart failure; (2) cancer; (3) kidney disease; and (4) liver disease. Early detection can lead to better treatment that can lengthen and improve the quality of life for your oldster.

removal of the whole bladder. Because they reroute the ureters into the colon, a dog will pass urine along with stool and will need to do this every four hours or so because there is nowhere to store it. A special diet and long-term antibiotics are also necessary. In some cases, a permanent urinary catheter can be installed to make urination easier for the dog. This won't stop the growth of the cancer, but it can make him more comfortable. Radiation therapy and drugs also have been used with this cancer, with inconsistent results.

CARDIOVASCULAR DISORDERS

The cardiovascular system is responsible for circulating blood throughout the body and consists of the heart and blood vessels. The heart is a powerful muscle located in the chest between the lungs, extending roughly between the third and sixth rib. It's contained in a very thin pericardial sac. The heart is the central pumping station of the body, and it consists of four "chambers": the right and left ventricle, and the right and left atrium. The atria "collect" blood, and the ventricles push it out. As dogs age, the heart muscles and walls weaken and can cause blood not to move well through the heart or to leak back into another chamber.

Heart disease is the leading cause of death in older dogs.

Senior small-breed dogs are most at risk of congestive heart failure.

General Signs

The main signs of heart disease in dogs are fatigue and exercise intolerance. Some may cough, especially at night. Your vet can usually detect a problem when she listens to the heart.

Pacemakers

Pacemakers are now available for dogs whose heart rate is too fast, too slow, or irregular. Most dog pacemakers were originally designed for people but were discarded for some minor defect that doesn't really affect their value to dogs. They usually work for 7 to 15 years, which just about covers it for a doggy life.

General Treatment

Fortunately, your vet has an arsenal of new devices and drugs to treat and prevent heart disease. These include electrocardiograms, ultrasounds (echocardiograms), and more.

Common Heart Problems

About 30 percent of older dogs have noticeable heart problems, especially congestive heart failure, enlarged hearts, heart murmurs, and heart rhythm disturbances.

Congestive Heart Failure (CHF)

As dogs age, the heart may lose its ability to contract and will fail to produce enough oxygenated blood for the other organs. In most cases, this occurs because of valve disease, arrhythmia, or plain old muscle failure. The dog will soon suffer from a buildup of fluids in the lungs. (Remember, the heart is basically a pump, and when pumps don't work right, fluid accumulates.) Small-breed dogs are most at risk.

Signs

The three main signs of this problem are labored breathing, exercise intolerance, and coughing. The heart rate of the dog may be too rapid, too slow, or irregular. There may be a loud heart murmur, but not all dogs with heart murmurs have heart failure.

Treatment

Your vet may prescribe a diuretic to remove fluid backup, as well as vasodilators and digitalis to make the heart beat stronger and more regularly. A low-salt diet is commonly prescribed as well. Good treatment can increase the life of your dog by months or even years.

Enlarged Heart

As the name suggests, an enlarged heart is one that is larger than normal. It occurs when it has to work extra hard because of an abnormality. An enlarged heart usually occurs along with heart failure.

SIGNS

There are no specific signs of an enlarged heart. Only a veterinarian can determine if one exists. Signs such as exercise intolerance and fatigue typically accompany conditions that cause the enlarged heart.

TREATMENT

An enlarged heart is often a result of congestive heart failure. Treatment often includes vasodilator drugs (ACE inhibitors), which open up the veins to help blood flow more easily, and diuretics, which reduce the blood volume so that the heart doesn't have to work as hard.

Heart Murmur

In older dogs, the mitral valve (located between the left atrium and the left ventricle and designed to prevent blood "backflow") may begin to leak, allowing blood to flow backward into the left atrium, a process that is called a heart murmur and that can eventually lead to heart failure. In short, a heart murmur is really a kind of vibration that is caused by disturbed blood flow.

A heart murmur can be caused by anemia, atrial septal defect, heartworm disease, cardiomyopathy, or a host of other diseases.

SIGNS

The signs of a murmur are specific heart noises that can be heard by your vet. These noises are graded from 1 to 6 and occur in different parts of the cardiac cycle. In some cases, heart murmurs are harmless; in others, they may be associated with more serious problems, and the dog may experience fatigue, coughing, and exercise intolerance.

TREATMENT

Your vet will probably treat your dog for heart failure if the murmur is serious. If the murmur is not serious, there is no treatment necessary.

Heart Rhythm Disturbance (Arrhythmia)

Arrhythmic is a term used to describe a heart that beats too fast, too slow, or irregularly. It is more common in large-breed dogs with an enlarged left atrium of the heart. Some arrhythmias are "benign" and require no particular therapy. Others are severe and can even lead to sudden death. An ECG is needed for diagnosis.

SIGNS

The sign of heart arrhythmia is a heartbeat that is too fast, too slow, or irregular. Your veterinarian can detect heart arrhythmia in your senior.

TREATMENT

Treatment depends on the cause, but in some cases, pacemakers (made for humans but donated to dogs) can be used. Your veterinarian also may prescribe medications designed to help.

EAR PROBLEMS

Ear problems are one of the most common complaints seen by veterinarians and include itchy ears, smelly ears, infected ears, dirty ears, bloody ears, and crusty ears. While senior dogs may be no more prone to ear problems than other dogs, they are extremely common in dogs of all ages.

Of all these conditions, ear infections are so common in dogs that fully 9 percent of all veterinary visits are for this condition. This is not really a surprising statistic—ears are warm, moist, and dark, the perfect place to harbor yeast and bacteria. Most ear infections are of the outer ear (not the ear flap itself, but the first part of the ear canal). If left untreated, the infection can migrate to the middle or even the inner ear.

Dogs with heavy, floppy ears face an even greater challenge because their ears are even warmer, wetter, and darker. And some breeds, like Cocker Spaniels, have a really long ear canal that "folds in" on itself before it reaches the eardrum. In any case, ear infections are nasty and very painful for your poor pooch.

Signs

Signs of ear problems include:

- head shaking

Scratching or pawing at the ears can be a sign of an ear infection.

- normally erect ears that droop
- redness or inflammation
- scratching or rubbing at the ears
- smelly ears
- swelling or discharge from the ears
- pain or avoidance on the dog's part when you try to stroke or examine the ears

⪻ Senior Moment ⪼

Feeding Tips

Make sure that your senior dog gets his own bowl to eat from and peace and quiet while eating. Doing so will encourage him to eat slower and help him avoid a host of digestive problems—from flatulence to bloat.

For older dogs, scratching at the ears may signal something even more serious than a run-of-the-mill infection—it could be a tumor. In many cases, the tumor is actually visible inside the ear canal, but your vet will want to X-ray or biopsy it for a complete analysis. Many of these tumors are benign.

Treatment

Treatment depends on the cause of the problem and may include cleaning the ear canal under sedation, topical ointments or sprays, and oral antibiotics for ten days. However, ear infections are notoriously difficult to treat. Part of the problem is the anatomy of the canine ear—it's L-shaped, and getting past the "junction" is difficult. Another problem is the nature of the infecting organism, whether bacterial or fungal. Fungi and bacteria respond to different treatment, so it is important for your vet to know the causative agent so that she can prescribe the right medication. Some commons medications now are broad spectrum and attempt to get the more common bacterial and fungus agent in one "shot," so to speak. In some cases, surgery is the best or only option. Several different procedures are available, but all are designed to remove the infected tissue and dry out the affected area.

After successful treatment, your older dog will be a like new creature. He will heal quickly, and you'll be surprised at his renewed life and energy.

ENDOCRINE SYSTEM DISORDERS

The endocrine system is a system of glands. It secretes hormones, steroids, and other chemicals that the body needs to function properly. Important organs in the endocrine system include the hypothalamus, pituitary gland, and thyroid gland.

- **Hypothalamus:** The hypothalamus is located in the brain. It issues hormones that stimulate or inhibit the pituitary gland to secrete hormones, which in turn directly or indirectly control growth and reproduction, fluid and electrolyte balance, and insulin production.

- **Pituitary gland:** The pituitary gland is a pea-sized gland attached to the base of the brain. It links the nervous system and endocrine system and releases many important hormones, such as the growth hormone that stimulates the adrenal gland, the thyroid-stimulating hormone that controls the thyroid, and several hormones that control the testes or ovaries. It even releases the hormone that affects skin color.

- **Thyroid gland:** The thyroid gland, located in the throat, controls metabolism and makes glucose and fats available for energy.

The endocrine system functions less effectively in older dogs, and so endocrine disorders are more common.

Cushing's Disease (Hyperadrenocorticism)

Most of the time, Cushing's develops because of tiny tumors in the pituitary gland. The tumors make the gland produce too much of a special hormone (ACTH) that in turn makes the adrenal glands overproduce cortisol, a hormone that regulates mineral metabolism.

Cushing's is a common condition of aging dogs (the mean age of onset is 8.5 years), and its signs are superficially like natural aging, with wrinkled skin, hair loss, and a potbelly, so it may escape your notice entirely.

Signs

There are quite a few signs of Cushing's disease, including the following:

- **Abnormal thirst and urination:** Normally dogs drink about 1 cup (236.6 ml) of water per day for each 10 pounds (4.5 kg) of body weight. Some dogs will have to go out in the middle of night to urinate, even when they never did before. Because this is also a sign

Panting that occurs even when it's not hot is typical of dogs who have Cushing's disease.

of diabetes and other illnesses, as well as a result of some medications like prednisone, this sign alone is not enough to diagnose the disease.

- **Hair loss:** Symmetrical hair loss along the sides of the body is the first obvious sign of Cushing's.

- **Increased appetite:** This will be so bad that many previously polite dogs will start stealing food from garbage cans or picking up nasty things in the yard or on the street to eat.

- **Muscle weakness:** This sign will be generalized over the whole body: Dogs become weak, lethargic, and unwilling to climb stairs.

- **Panting:** Panting that occurs even when it is not hot is common. Cushing's dogs seem unable to control their body temperature.

- **Potbelly:** This is present in 90 percent of dogs with Cushing's and will occur even though the dog is not overweight. The potbelly results from the redistribution of body fat in addition to a breakdown of abdominal musculature.

- **Skin disease:** Many Cushing's dogs exhibit signs of skin disease, which are caused by hormonal factors. These include symmetrical hair loss on the trunk or hair that doesn't regrow after clipping; thin, wrinkled skin with poor wound healing; skin darkening and blemishes on the skin, especially the abdomen; persistent skin infections; hard little rock-like areas all over the body; and calcium deposits on the skin.

- **Urinary tract infections:** Dogs with Cushing's are more likely to come down with urinary tract infections, which may be hard to detect because the urine is diluted. (Recent studies show that 20 percent of Cushing's dogs have an "inapparent" bladder infection.)

Your vet can detect Cushing's disease with the highly accurate "low-dose dexamethasone suppression test," which requires an eight-hour hospital stay. This test, which measures cortisol levels, is considered the best, with a 90 to 95 percent accuracy rate. The "adrenocorticotrophic hormone," or "ACTH," stimulation test is also sometimes used, which measures the response of the adrenal glands to a high dose of ACTH.

Diagnosing Cushing's

The signs of Cushing's are quite similar to those of natural aging and so often escape notice.

Treatment

Treatment depends on the type of Cushing's disease present—whether it is pituitary or adrenal based—and the general health of the patient. It may include chemotherapy for pituitary- or adrenal-based Cushing's, or surgery for adrenal-based Cushing's.

Unfortunately, even with good treatment, most Cushing's dogs live only about two years after diagnosis. However, treatment vastly improves the quality of the dog's life during that time. If not treated, Cushing's will progress. Early intervention can lengthen your dog's life.

Diabetes Mellitus

About 1 in every 200 dogs will develop diabetes, with most dogs between seven and nine years of age at the time of diagnosis. A dog suffering from diabetes has a deficiency of or insensitivity to insulin, a hormone produced in the islet cells of the pancreas. Both too much or too little of this critical substance is lethal because insulin controls blood concentrations of glucose (blood sugar), the main fuel for the body. Insulin also controls the amount of glucose in the blood by preventing overproduction by the liver and ensures that excess glucose derived from food and not needed for energy is put into body stores. However, dogs with diabetes do not have enough insulin to switch off the liver's glucose production or to efficiently store excess glucose derived from foods. The glucose may simply rampage through the bloodstream without getting to the cells.

Signs

Signs of diabetes include:

- excessive urination
- increased appetite and thirst
- skin problems
- weakness
- weight loss (despite a good appetite)

As diabetes gets worse, toxic glucose metabolites accumulate, causing vomiting, dehydration, and eventual death.

What Causes Diabetes?

Dogs who suffer from diabetes have a deficiency of or insensitivity to insulin.

Treatment

This common disease can be managed (although not cured) with early diagnosis and proper treatment. It may be helpful to supplement with an antioxidant such as vitamin E, which may minimize the breakdown of fats in the body. Regular, moderate exercise is also important.

Diabetes often can be treated successfully by getting the dog to a proper weight and following the general dietary guidelines, which start with feeding a nutritionally complete and balanced food with a consistent proportion of carbohydrates, fats, and proteins. Fat should be restricted to 20 percent of calories, and high-quality protein sources should be used. Diabetic dogs of normal or above-normal weight should consume a moderate amount of fiber. You can add fiber to your dog's normal dog food using a fiber source such as psyllium or canned pumpkin. You also may elect to buy a commercial food that already contains the proper quantities of fiber.

Dogs with advanced diabetes need regular doses of insulin, often twice a day. While you may be squeamish about giving it at first, the needle is so fine that your dog will probably not even notice that he is being given a shot. Your vet can show you how to administer the injection.

Many factors, such as exercise levels, can influence how much insulin your dog needs on a day-to-day basis. You can safely monitor your dog's glucose at home—only a little bit of blood is required, and you can extract it from his ear. A new device is available that lances the skin and creates a vacuum that collects the required blood within 30 seconds. You also can use urine test strips to check blood sugar levels of glucose. A portable monitor will measure the results for either method.

Regularly scheduled meals are important when administering insulin. If you're away at mealtime, you can purchase a timed feeder set to the regular feeding hour. A dog receiving insulin twice a day should ideally receive four meals a day: one at the time of each insulin injection, one in the early afternoon, and one in the late evening.

Hypoglycemia

Following an insulin injection, diabetic dogs can suffer from hypoglycemia, a condition in which their blood sugar levels drop radically. Small dogs, especially when they are puppies, are most prone to this condition. Hypoglycemic dogs appear confused; they may even have a seizure. If this happens, rub a bit of honey or syrup on your dog's gums.

Many factors, such as exercise levels, can influence how much insulin a diabetic dog needs on a day-to-day basis.

Hypothyroidism

Hypothyroidism is a disorder in which the thyroid gland does not secrete enough thyroid hormone, which is critical to regulating your dog's metabolic rate. As a result, cells don't convert food energy into biologically usable fuel quickly enough. A dog can lose 30 percent of his thyroid function between the ages of 3 and 11.

Signs

Almost half of hypothyroid dogs gain weight, even with no change in diet. A sizable percentage also becomes lethargic and mentally slow. Hair- and skin-producing cells slow down, so there is less hair growth and more hair loss. Some dogs show increased aggression. In addition, hypothyroid dogs have an increased risk of joint and ligament disease. Because signs are variable and the disease develops gradually, it often goes undiagnosed.

Hypothyroidism typically develops in dogs who are middle aged and older, so be

Pancreatitis Risk Factors

Risk factors for pancreatitis include high fat content in the blood, obesity, infection, and contaminated food.

watchful for signs in your senior, and if you are suspicious, ask your vet to check for the disease. A simple blood test will give you the answer.

Treatment

Once diagnosed, hypothyroidism is easy to treat with a relatively inexpensive oral supplemental thyroid hormone administered once or twice a day. Once treatment begins, most affected dogs become increasingly active and show fewer problem behaviors within a week. Hair growth typically accelerates in about a week, too.

Pancreatitis

The pancreas is a little organ tucked up under the tummy and small intestine. It produces enzymes needed to digest food; it also produces hormones, including insulin. Pancreatitis occurs when the pancreas becomes inflamed and starts leaking those digestive enzymes—the organ can even start digesting itself. Some kinds of pancreatitis happen overnight, while others take a long time to develop. Both kinds can be painful and life threatening. Dogs of any age can be affected, but the disease is most common in dogs who are middle aged and older—especially obese females. Most affected animals are over seven years old.

Unfortunately, not much is known about what causes pancreatitis, although certain risk factors have been identified. These include high fat content in the blood, obesity, infection, contaminated food, pancreatic duct obstruction, certain other diseases like diabetes or Cushing's, and some drugs. This is a disease particularly common in older females.

Signs

Signs of pancreatitis include:

- abdomen that hurts when touched
- change in body temperature (either way)
- dehydration
- depression
- diarrhea
- food avoidance
- jaundice

- rapid heartbeat
- respiratory distress
- standing in a hunched position
- vomiting

None of these signs, however, is a sure sign of pancreatitis—the disease is notoriously hard to diagnose. Your vet will run tests that include a check on the pancreatic enzymes for more clues. She also may take X-rays, do an ultrasound, or administer a blood test.

Treatment

The only treatment for pancreatitis is supportive therapy, which usually includes intravenous feeding for a few days so that the digestive system can rest. Afterward, your senior will probably be placed on a low-fat diet. Special prescription diets are available.

EYE PROBLEMS

Just as with people, dogs can expect to develop eye problems as they age. Eyesight dims, the lens thickens, and other degenerative changes occur. The lens may get cloudy or bluish. In most cases, this is nothing to worry about, but the other conditions mentioned in this section require immediate attention.

Eye problems in dogs run the gamut from nothing to worry about to extremely serious. Distinguishing one from another requires a veterinarian.

General Signs

Sign	Potential Cause
irritated and painful-looking eyes	entropion, other irritation
squinting, scratching, or pawing at eye	corneal ulcer, glaucoma, irritation
gray or cloudy eyes	cataracts, glaucoma, lenticular sclerosis
seems blind	cataracts, glaucoma, progressive retinal atrophy
bloodshot eyes	allergies, foreign object, glaucoma, tumor
eyes that have discharge for 48 hours or more	entropion, infection, scratched cornea, seasonal allergy

bulging eyes	glaucoma, infection, prolapsed eyeball, tumor
eyelids swollen or unable to close	allergic reaction, infection
growth on eye or eyelid	benign but could be a tumor, bite, allergic reaction
one or both pupils dilated or unresponsive to light	antifreeze poisoning, nerve damage, tumor
red "lump" in eye	cherry eye
eyes oversensitive to light	anterior uveitis, iris atrophy
droopy or sunken eyes	Horner's syndrome
third eyelids apparent, covering lower parts of eyes	may be dust or dirt in the eye
continuous darting of eyes back and forth	probably a neurological problem
blood or tiny blood vessels visible in the center (not the whites) of eyes	injury
eyelid appears to be turned inward	entropion
eyelid appears to be turned outward	ectropion

The best rule is to have any abnormality of the eyes or adjacent tissues evaluated by a vet without delay. Waiting even a few hours could cost your dog his vision.

General Treatment
Your vet will treat the eye problem according to its cause. Treatment may include applying a soothing or cleansing lotion, irrigating the eye, antibiotics, or surgery.

Common Eye Problems
Some of the most common eye problems in seniors include cataracts, dry eye, glaucoma, and lenticular nuclear sclerosis.

Cataracts

A cataract is an opacity of the lens. Although it looks as if the cloudiness is just on the surface, the occluded lens lies deeper within the eye. Most cataracts are inherited, with Cocker Spaniels, Poodles, Siberian Huskies, Schnauzers, Golden Retrievers, Labrador Retrievers, and many kinds of terriers most at risk. Other causes include diabetes, trauma, and inflammation.

SIGNS

Signs include gradual visual loss, reluctance to go out at night, and cloudy lens.

TREATMENT

Just as with people, cataracts can be treated by surgical removal. The success rate for this surgery is more than 90 percent, but as with any surgery, there are risks. There are two basic kinds of surgery, depending on the size of cataract and other factors. A small incision technique (phacoemulsification) is suitable for most dogs; it has the benefits of being a shorter surgery with a quicker healing time. A tiny probe breaks up the cataract with ultrasonic vibration and draws out the cataract particles. Other dogs may need a larger incision technique (extracapsular cataract extraction), involving removal of the hard nucleus of the cataract. After removal of the cataract your ophthalmologist may suggest replacement of the lens with an artificial lens, which will give your dog better vision.

You will have to be a very hands-on and committed owner after cataract surgery; you will need to give eye drops several times daily for several weeks both before and after the surgery. Also, your dog must wear an Elizabethan collar, and that can be a hassle for both of you.

It should be noted that cataracts aren't painful, and most dogs do very well after going blind. They depend less on sight than on their other senses anyway and soon learn to find their way around. Sometimes dogs go blind gradually, and it may be years before their owners even realize it.

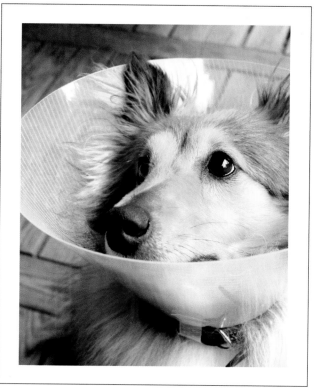

Your dog will have to wear an Elizabethan collar after cataract surgery.

Distinguishing one eye condition from another requires a veterinarian's expertise.

Dry Eye

As dogs age, they tend to get drier eyes. A dog with dry eye does not produce enough tears, which results in a dry and painful eye. (This can be tested by your vet with a tear test.)

SIGNS
There may be thick, stringy discharge from one or both eyes. Eventually there will be changes in the cornea.

TREATMENT
Your vet can give you special drops to help the condition, and there are several on the market that can help to keep senior eyes moist. With serious cases of dry eye, cyclosporine is usually prescribed.

Glaucoma

Glaucoma is the most common cause of blindness in dogs. It is a painful condition in which the pressure inside the eyeball increases to dangerous levels and damages the optic nerve because the drainage sites are too narrow. Certain breeds, such as Cocker Spaniels, are at increased risk of developing glaucoma.

While both people and dogs can get glaucoma, there's an important difference. With people, the disease usually progresses slowly and often painlessly. With dogs, it may have a (literally) blindingly fast onset, is excruciatingly painful, and is a veterinary emergency.

SIGNS
Unfortunately, dogs are so stoic that you may not even know your dog has a problem unless you are alert for its signs: squinting, redness, and cloudiness. For a definitive diagnosis, your vet will need to take a medical history, measure the pressure within the eye, and perform a physical examination. In addition, medical tests are needed to establish the diagnosis and exclude other diseases. Your dog's eyes should be checked very carefully twice a year after the age of eight.

TREATMENT
Medical options for treating glaucoma include emergency and oral medications to

lower ocular pressure, medications to decrease the production of fluid in the eye and help to open the drainage angle, and anti-inflammatories to decrease inflammation in the eye. Surgical options include laser surgery, the implantation of a small tube in the eye to drain excess fluid, or complete eye removal.

In cases where the pressure has been caused by some physical plugging of the "drain" in the eye, like a tumor, chronic uveitis, or lens luxation, sight may be restored. With hereditary glaucoma, though, sight usually will eventually be lost in both eyes. However, the disease still needs to be treated, sometimes requiring the removal of the blind eye, to stop the pain.

Lenticular Nuclear Sclerosis

Most older dogs develop a fairly benign eye problem called lenticular nuclear sclerosis, which produces a bluish haze over the eyes but does not materially affect the vision. However, this harmless condition could be mistaken for cataracts by a nonexpert.

SIGNS

The lens may be cloudy or bluish.

TREATMENT

This is a normal sign of aging and does not cause significant vision loss. No treatment is necessary—or available.

GASTROINTESTINAL DISORDERS

The gastrointestinal (GI) system extracts and processes nutrients from food and passes waste from the body. The GI tract includes the mouth, teeth, tongue, pharynx,

---

Abscessed Carnassial Teeth

If you see a lump under the eye of your older dog, it may very well have resulted from an abscessed carnassial tooth (that's the fourth premolar). These lumps can get massive, up to the size of a golf ball! It may look like a badly infected insect bite or tumor, but its position on the face is a good clue as to its real origin. Dogs over the age of seven, especially those whose dental care has been neglected, are extremely prone to this condition.

The carnassial tooth is huge, with three strong roots. (Most teeth have only two.) Usually the infection involves only the root of the tooth. Once the infection-causing bacteria settles in between the root of the tooth and skull, it is almost impossible to get rid of without tooth extraction. Antibiotic treatment alone is only a temporary solution; the infection inevitably returns. Once the tooth is removed, the infection can be treated and your dog will be able to eat everything just as before.

SENIOR TALES

"Rowdy"

Sheila Boneham remembers, "One morning when he was about ten years old, my Australian Shepherd, Rowdy, acted as if he was bloating. He was restless, panting, and pacing the floor, and I could see that he was having abdominal contractions. We had moved to town recently, and I had only been to the new vet once previously, so I didn't know him very well. He in turn didn't know that I'm a very proactive owner when it comes to my animals' health care! Anyway, he told me on the phone that Aussies don't bloat (not true!) and that I should "wait and see how he does over the next few hours" (wrong again!). I told him that we were on our way in, and if he couldn't see me, someone would. He did see us and thought Rowdy was in respiratory distress. I insisted that he get one of the more experienced vets. It turned out that Rowdy was not yet bloating, but he did have a bad case of gas and a bad bellyache. He had broken his leg a few weeks earlier, and we suspect that when they took the cast off the day before, he licked it and ingested bacteria that caused the intestinal problem. The buildup of gas could easily have escalated to bloat and stomach torsion, which can be fatal. Fortunately, quick treatment relieved the gas pressure, and a course of antibiotics prevented a recurrence.

"It always pays to remember that vets, like medical doctors, are often rushed and may miss things. We have to ask questions, be observant, and sometimes, be pushy in defense of our dogs' health. After all, they would do the same for us."

esophagus, stomach, small intestine, and large intestine (colon). As dogs age, they may have higher numbers of unfavorable bacteria in the intestines and so may experience more gastrointestinal problems, including bloat, diarrhea and vomiting, flatulence, inflammatory bowel disease, and periodontal disease.

Bloat

Bloat is a serious medical emergency that, if untreated, always leads to painful death within hours. In this condition, the stomach becomes dilated with gas or fluids and twists on itself, blocking off blood flow to the stomach and other vital organs.

Dogs most vulnerable include breeds with deep, narrow chests such as Weimaraners, Great Danes, and Basset Hounds. Most at risk are thin dogs, anxious dogs, dogs who eat too fast, and older animals. In fact, a dog's chance of developing the disease increases with age, with dogs over the age of seven twice as likely to bloat as two-year-olds.

Signs

If your dog suddenly develops a distended belly, paces, salivates, tries to vomit unsuccessfully, or seems in pain and is getting worse, get him to an emergency vet immediately. *Do not wait* to seek treatment.

Treatment

Many clinical reports from Europe and the United States show that gastropexy, a procedure in which the stomach is attached to the body wall to prevent gastric rotation, should be performed as soon as possible following stomach decompression on all dogs

Dogs with deep, narrow chests, such as Weimaraners, are most at risk of bloat.

with bloat. The recurrence rate of bloat in dogs treated without this surgery approaches 100 percent. The recurrence rate following gastropexy is less than 5 percent.

To reduce your dog's chance of getting bloat, feed smaller and more frequent meals. Three meals a day is better than two. Statistics also show that adding a few tablespoons (ml) of healthy table scraps to his kibble will reduce the chances of his developing bloat. Avoid exercising your dog right after a meal.

Dental Disease

The American Veterinary Dental Society (AVDS) estimates that more than 80 percent of dogs and cats over the age of four show signs of oral disease, and the percentage increases with age.

If not treated, harmless-looking plaque buildup hardens and turns into tartar, a cement-like form of calcium carbonate. An ordinary toothbrush won't get rid of it. This

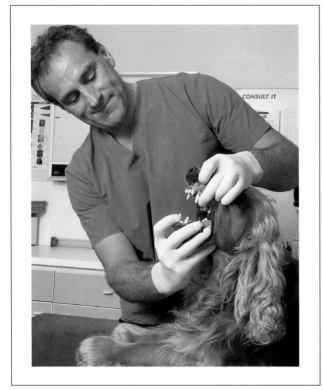

You can help to prevent dental disease with veterinary dental checks.

leads to numerous health problems, including bad breath and gingivitis, an inflammation of the gums usually caused by food particles packed into the crevices between the gums and teeth. These pockets favor the invasion of increasingly harmful types of bacteria. The gums become red, painful, and swollen and may begin bleeding or receding. If gingivitis is not treated, it may lead to periodontitis, a serious infection of the tissue and bone in which the teeth are rooted. Eventually, tooth loss occurs. Even more serious are the infections that may follow, potentially damaging the heart, liver, brain, and kidneys.

Signs

Signs of periodontal disease include bad breath, reluctance to chew, reddened, inflamed gums, and gums receding around the teeth.

Sadly, even if periodontal disease is severe, your dog may suffer in silence, showing no clinical signs of pain and continuing to eat even hard dry food simply by swallowing the kibble whole. If you aren't on the ball, you may not notice anything is wrong until all the teeth have become infected.

Treatment

Take a good look at your dog's teeth. If they are dirty, have them professionally cleaned. Even if your dog has serious dental disease, good dentistry can remove the sources of infection. During a professional cleaning, all calculus is removed from above and below the gum line. The teeth also will be polished, not for looks but to remove microscopic scratches that can harbor germs and plaque. Your pet might lose a few teeth in the process, but he will feel a lot better. Some specialists even do root canals!

Before the surgery, your vet may wish to put your dog on an oral antibiotic, especially if there is severe dental disease present. That is because these animals have many more oral bacteria, along with bleeding gums. This can be a deadly combination. Bacteria entering the bloodstream can build up on heart valves and in the internal organs, initiating a lethal infection. The antibiotics are designed to keep this from happening.

Prevention is the best way to go when it comes to dental disease. Many things can go wrong with the teeth and gums, but you can prevent almost all of them with regular brushing and veterinary dental checks.

Diarrhea and Vomiting

It is an unfortunate fact of life that two of the most unpleasant signs of gastrointestinal distress—diarrhea and vomiting—are also the commonest. They are not diseases in themselves but signs that something else is wrong. The something wrong would be dietary indiscretion, parasite infection, or a life-threatening condition. Because senior dogs have less reserve than healthy young adults do, their signs need to be taken seriously.

Signs

A little diarrhea or vomiting is not uncommon in dogs, but there are certain signals that tell you when to take your oldster to the vet:

- the dog vomits blood or a black coffee-ground-like substance
- diarrhea or vomiting lasts for two days
- the dog has a fever of over 102.5°F (39.2°C)
- diarrhea is bloody or black
- the dog refuses food
- the dog is becoming dehydrated (check to see if the gums are sticky
- the dog has other signs of illness

Treatment

If your dog has a simple case of diarrhea or vomiting, put him on a fast. (The dog may have small drinks of water only to prevent fluid loss.) Do not feed anything—including a so-called "bland" diet—for 24 hours. This will give the gastrointestinal tract time to heal itself. If the situation does not resolve by the next day, or if there is blood in the vomit or stool, contact your vet.

Flatulence

You usually can diagnose flatulence if you look to the cause. The most common causes include eating too fast, eating gas-producing food like beans, and eating a poor-quality food that is loaded with carbs and low on protein.

Signs

Flatulence makes itself known by its smell—there are usually no other signs.

Treatment

To take care of the problem, divide your dog's food into smaller portions and let him eat in a quiet, undisturbed room in the hope that he will slow down if not fearing that someone else will grab his dinner. Frequent exercise also gets those intestines working better and diminishes the possibility of gas. In addition, select a good-quality dog food, preferably one without corn, which often causes this condition.

If the flatulence does not resolve, check with your vet. There are products containing digestives enzymes that are available to help this condition.

Inflammatory Bowel Disease (IBD)

IBD is a common ailment in dogs, primarily affecting dogs over the age of two, but the actual cause is still somewhat mysterious. Current thinking is that it is an overreaction to normal bacteria in the intestine, causing the immune system to go into a kind of "overdrive."

IBD causes intermittent diarrhea or vomiting in a classic waxing and waning pattern. About a third of the sufferers have only vomiting or only diarrhea. The inflammation may be in the stomach, small intestine, large intestine—or all three.

Signs

Signs include acute or chronic intermittent vomiting or intermittent diarrhea. Weight loss is common. Some animals may have poor coat quality. Some appear depressed.

Treatment

Therapy usually consists of controlling the inflammation as well as trying to eliminate the cause. Treatment depends on the cause or causes. Common suspects include dietary components such as meat proteins, artificial coloring, preservatives, milk proteins, and wheat gluten. Dogs with IBD are often given diets in which these ingredients are not present.

Dogs diagnosed with IBD may now have an effective alternative treatment: Most veterinarians prescribe a bland diet that won't aggravate the disease. However, while a change in diet may be helpful, the most effective way to control IBD in the past has been with the use of steroids. The problem is that not all dogs respond to this treatment, and even those who do sometimes experience serious side effects.

IMMUNE SYSTEM DISEASES

The immune system is a whole network of organs and specialized cells that work to defend the body from pathogens. It "recognizes" foreign invaders. When such invaders appear, the immune system goes into action to fight them off. Unfortunately, the immune system is weaker in seniors than it is in young adults and may need your help.

Allergies

Like people, dogs can suffer from allergies: household mold, dust mites, fleas, pollen, and even substances in food. Anything that causes an allergy is called an allergen.

An allergy is really a hypersensitive immune reaction. The immune system is designed to ratchet up into high gear when faced with a dangerous pathogen, but sometimes, in some individuals, the immune system mistakes a harmless substance like tree pollen for a killer disease. It kicks in with everything it has, and instead of repelling the invader, it makes the host as sick as—well, as a dog.

Signs

Dogs with allergies lick their feet, rub their faces, chew their legs, and scratch at their "armpits." Many develop related skin or ear problems.

Treatment

In all cases of allergy, the sooner you start treatment, the better. In a few cases, switching to a high-quality diet may help, but if your dog is allergic to something like pollen, it doesn't matter what he eats. However, the addition of fatty acids to the diet, hypoallergenic shampoos, and oatmeal-based topical treatments may help the symptoms. Fatty acids, especially omega-3 fatty acids from fish oil, are often helpful.

Topical medications will soothe hot spots and ear infections, although sometimes your vet may need to resort to antibiotics and antifungals. The next step may be antihistamines, then skin testing and allergy shots.

In addition, you may want to try some holistic alternatives, such as high doses of

Anaphylaxis

The most serious response to an allergy is anaphylaxis, a rare but life-threatening reaction—usually to something injected, like bee venom or a vaccination, but on occasion to something ingested. Signs of anaphylaxis include sudden onset diarrhea, vomiting, seizures, shock, and coma. The heart rate is fast, but the pulse is weak. Gums are often pale, and the limbs feel cold.

If you think that your dog is having an anaphylactic reaction, get *immediate* veterinary help; a few minutes can spell the difference between life and death. Your vet will administer epinephrine, IV fluids, and oxygen.

If your older dog is having trouble climbing up stairs or even getting up on the couch as easily as he once did, he may have arthritis.

vitamin C (which has an antihistamine effect). Other suggestions include B-carotene, quercetin (a bioflavonoid), vitamin E, and selenium. Herbs that are sometimes used include yellow dock, nettles, calendula, and licorice. You also might look into trying Chinese herbs; they often are more effective than Western herbs for this purpose. Talk with your vet if you decide to try a holistic alternative.

Immune-Mediated Anemia (IMHA)

Immune-mediated anemia (IMHA) is a disease in which the body's immune system kills its own red blood cells. This is a life-threatening situation. The causes of IMHA remain largely unknown, although several "suspects" have been suggested, including infections, cancers, and overvaccination. Cocker Spaniels, Springer Spaniels, Poodles, and Old English Sheepdogs seem most at risk.

Signs

Signs include the typical symptoms of anemia: pale gums, yellow-tinged eye whites, dark urine, and lethargy. Your vet will do a complete blood count, reticulocyte count (a count of a special type of red blood cell), and packed cell volume test to help diagnose the problem. Other tests also may be appropriate.

Treatment

Treatment goals for this disease include the improvement of oxygen delivery to cells, hydration, and immunosuppression. For the last, the main therapy for IMHA is the administration of corticosteroids like prednisone. These drugs suppress the immune system's ability to attack its own cells. More severe cases call for stronger drugs. Some veterinarians recommend removal of the spleen, which is often working abnormally, in cases that fail to respond to medical treatment. This is an invasive technique that is seldom performed, although it has achieved a high degree of success.

MUSCULOSKELETAL SYSTEM DISORDERS

The skeleton is your dog's bony framework, consisting of bones, ligaments, tendons, and cartilage. Its main job is to support the body, protect soft tissues, store minerals and fat, and enable movement. After a lifetime of playing catch, running up and down stairs, and just having a good time, the older dog's system shows some stress, just as a human's does.

Arthritis

Virtually every old dog will get arthritis, a degenerative bone disease that affects cartilage, bone, and surrounding soft tissues. In the United States, about 1/5 of the 55 million dogs in the United States are being treated for this condition. So it's safe to say that if you own an older dog, he has at least some degree of arthritis.

The word "arthritis" is often used for a whole range of degenerative joint diseases found in dogs, including hip dysplasia, osteochondritis, osteoarthritis, and various spinal conditions, all of which produce arthritic changes in the body. This section will mostly cover degenerative joint disease, the form most universally seen. This type of arthritis can be treated fairly satisfactorily without resorting to expensive surgery or other heroic measures, which is not the case with hip dysplasia or certain other conditions caused by structural malformations.

As dogs age, the cartilage that protects the ends of bones becomes less resilient, heals more slowly, and is more likely to break

Overweight Dogs and Arthritis

Overweight dogs are much more likely to suffer from arthritis than their thinner counterparts are. Keep your dog trim!

down. As it wears away, the ends of the bone come into direct contact and can grind against each other, resulting in painful inflammation. This process is progressive and incurable, although it is amenable to treatment.

The main causes of arthritis are:

- breed disposition (certain lines of Labradors Retrievers, Golden Retrievers, and German Shepherds are more prone to the condition)
- diseases including Lyme disease and Rocky Mountain spotted fever
- joint abnormalities
- joint trauma
- obesity (the more obese the dog, the worse the arthritis)
- overactivity in certain canine sports

Arthritis usually first appears in dogs between the ages of five and eight.

Signs

Signs of arthritis include lameness, stiffness, reluctance to negotiate stairs, and difficulty lying down or getting up. However, some dogs show advanced stages of arthritis on X-rays but barely limp. Maybe they are trying to "cover it up" by pretending not to be hurting. In these dogs, signs may be very subtle. A dog can feel a great deal of pain without giving outward indications of it. On the other hand, other dogs show extreme pain and stiffness, although an X-ray reveals little actual damage. Pain perception is a personal thing.

Treatment

Arthritis is not curable, but different treatments are available, including:

- **Antioxidants:** Antioxidants "scavenge" free radicals that damage cartilage and other tissue. If you go this route, use only antioxidants formulated at human-grade level. Antioxidants have an anti-inflammatory function and can lessen the pain associated with arthritis. The best choices contain

Signs of Lameness

If your dog shows signs of lameness, do not just assume that it's arthritis and so can wait for treatment. It may be bone cancer. If you can catch it before it metastasizes, there are good treatment options available. Take your dog to the vet for a thorough examination.

proanthocyanidins from pine bark or grape seed extract (or meal) and bioflavonoids. Bioflavonoids are plant substances with recognized antioxidant properties and the ability to inhibit the activity of certain enzymes that cause inflammation in the body.

Moderate exercise, such as swimming, helps to keep the joints moving fluidly and prevents them from stiffening up.

- **Controlled exercise:** Moderate exercise keeps the joints moving more fluidly and prevents them from stiffening up. Too much exercise puts stress on the joints. (If you can get your dog to a pool, that's one of the best exercises of all.)

- **Hip or knee surgery:** Damaged cartilage can be shaved off, and abnormal bone tissue can be trimmed. This treatment allows the dog to move freely again.

- **Massage:** Massage helps to support the muscles and gets the circulation going. Done right, it provides range of motion to the joints.

- **Nonsteroidal anti-inflammatory drugs (NSAIDs):** NSAIDs work within a couple of weeks to reduce inflammation. Use drugs meant for dogs, not people. It's also important to remember that any drug can cause adverse reactions to the gastrointestinal system, especially over time. Frequent testing may be necessary to make sure that the liver remains healthy.

- **Nutraceuticals:** A nutraceutical is a substance that acts something like a food and something like a drug but is not technically either one. Examples of nutraceuticals include chondroitin, glucosamine, manganese, and omega-3 fatty acids. They can be effective but take several weeks to work. In addition, not all over-the-counter products are equal (despite their label claims), especially when it comes to chondroitin and glucosamine. Ask your vet for a pharmaceutical-grade product for optimum effectiveness.

- **Physical therapy:** Physical therapy uses a variety of techniques to increase a dog's range of motion and develop his strength.

- **Polysulfated glycosaminoglycan (PSGAG):** PSGAG not only promotes cartilage growth but also repairs cartilage damage and helps to prevent injury by inhibiting enzymes responsible for the breakdown of the various joint components. This drug can be injected intramuscularly. A typical course of treatment is eight shots administered a few days apart.

Age-Defying Tip

Old Age . . . or Something Else?

If your older dog suddenly appears to go off his food, hide, shake, or seem "depressed," do not assume it is old age. He may be suffering from something physical rather than existential angst. Have him checked out by your vet so that the problem can be treated.

Just as important as what the vet can do are changes you can make at home. Weight control; a pleasant environment; a comfortable bed; mild, regular exercise; and ice packs to soothe swollen joints all can make your senior feel much better.

Diskospondylitis

This is a disease of the spine that originates from a bacterial or fungal infection of the vertebral disks. Bigger, older dogs are most frequently affected, with Great Danes leading the list.

Signs

Signs include pain, fever, listlessness, and sometimes paralysis.

Treatment

Treatment consists of pain medication, rest, and antibiotics to cure the condition.

Herniated Discs

As dogs get older, the protective cushions between the vertebrae, called spinal discs, tend to grow weaker, especially in long-backed breeds like Dachshunds. If a disc ruptures, the jelly-like material inside will ooze out, possibly putting pressure on a spinal nerve.

Signs

Signs include acute pain, a "drunken" walk, or paralysis. The specific sign depends on which disc has herniated.

Treatment

In some cases, herniated discs may resolve with crate rest; in other cases, decompression surgery is required. Physical therapy is also very helpful

NERVOUS SYSTEM DISORDERS

The nervous system is your dog's headquarters. The brain, which gathers and sends out information, is the boss. It governs all behavior and produces nerve impulses. The spinal cord, together with the cranial nerves, is the second-in-command, transmitting the brain's directions to the rest of the body. It is important in senior dogs to recognize that many nervous system problems are just that—problems in and of themselves—not generalized signs of old age.

Canine Cognitive Disorder

This condition is generally defined as a syndrome associated with brain aging that is unrelated to any other condition. The onset is gradual. The older your dog, the more likely he is to be a victim of CCD. No one knows why an individual dog may come down with CCD, although it's thought that inheritance probably plays a role.

Signs

Signs of CCD include:

- confusion

- less responsive and may act as if he doesn't recognize you

- seems to get "stuck" in a corner, unable to figure out how to extricate himself

- increased thirst

- loss of housetraining

- separation anxiety

- sleeping all day and barking all night

A few dogs may show aggression to other dogs or to people.

While technically a different disease from Alzheimer's disease in people, the pathological changes that occur in the brain of affected dogs are quite similar to those of Alzheimer's patients.

Treatment

CCD is progressive, but it is also treatable, a fact that

Did You Know?

Canine cognitive disorder affects a dog's brain similar to how Alzheimer's affects a human's brain.

A dog with canine cognitive disorder may act confused and be less responsive in general.

comes as a surprise to many who think that disorientation and strange behavior are inevitable parts of old age. Remember that CCD is a disease—it's not "normal" for an older dog to experience this dysfunction.

Medication (selegiline) is available that can reverse many of the signs of the disease. It increases the brain's concentrations of dopamine, a neurotransmitter that connects thought to action and increases cognitive awareness. About one-third of dogs respond extremely well to this therapy, another third responds reasonably well, and the remaining third do not respond at all. For more information, contact your veterinarian, who will want to give your dog a thorough examination and make a determination if medication is worth a try with your senior.

There is also strong evidence that the proper diet can prevent or substantially delay the onset of CCD. (For more information, see Chapter 3.)

Epilepsy and Other Seizure Disorders

Epilepsy is a neurological disease characterized by sudden, recurring seizures caused by abnormal electrical activity in the brain. A seizure is a condition in which the neurons fire abnormally, causing body responses ranging from mild twitches to serious convulsions. Causes of seizures can include tumors, cardiovascular disease, metabolic disorders, toxins, infections, and even low blood sugar.

Seizures can occur in any dog of any age, but if your senior is not epileptic and suddenly starts having seizures, it is a veterinary emergency.

Signs

Some dogs give subtle signs that a seizure is approaching and have altered behavior. They may appear confused or may lick their lips in apparent nervousness. During the actual seizure, the animal will lose consciousness, sometimes completely, sometimes only partially. He may move his legs as though running and twitch and shake. Some dogs salivate, others pass urine or feces. It is a frightening thing, but there is nothing you can do in the way of first aid to shorten or lessen the seizure, other than darkening the room and moving furniture out of the way.

After the seizure, the dog will appear confused. He also may exhibit behavioral changes for some time afterward.

Treatment
Classical epilepsy usually strikes younger dogs, but because there is no cure for the disease, once epileptic, always epileptic. It is a condition that usually requires lifelong medication. If your previously normal older dog suddenly begins to have seizures, look for an explanation.

Old Dog Vestibular Disease
The "vestibular equipment" in dogs is what helps them keep their balance and what helps them move around without getting dizzy. These special receptors are located in the middle ear, which contains canals of fluid. There are tiny little hair cells that project into this fluid and wave around in there, transmitting important balance information to the brain, which in turn gives instructions to the leg and eye muscles to help a dog balance. In older dogs, something may go awry with the system, at least temporarily. Often the precipitating factors are not known, although an infection is sometimes involved, especially if the dog has a history of ear infections. In the most serious cases, a brain tumor could be present.

Signs
Dogs with this problem usually tilt their heads to one side. They may walk in a drunken or circular way or may vomit from "motion sickness." Their eyes may dart around in an aimless or back-and-forth motion. In some cases, they may even fall to one side.

Treatment
This scary situation usually rights itself (literally) within 72 hours. The dog simply gets used to the altered signals and compensates. If he does not, your vet may

Some dogs give subtle signs that a seizure is approaching, such as lip licking.

Your vet can help you keep your senior dog happy and healthy.

want to do an imaging of the middle ear and treat for infection. There could be a connection between this condition and hypothyroidism, so your vet may want to check your dog's thyroid function as well.

RESPIRATORY SYSTEM DISORDERS

The respiratory system allows your dog to breathe. It consists of the nasal passages, nasopharynx (the back of the mouth), the voice box (larynx), the windpipe (trachea), the lower airway passages (bronchi), and the lungs. An older, less efficient respiratory system makes a senior dog more likely to fall prey to various problems.

Kennel Cough (Bordetellosis)

Kennel cough is a condition that can be caused by several pathogens that team up and damage the lining of the trachea and bronchi, exposing the nerve endings. The disease gets its name from the fact that most victims are confined in close quarters at a shelter or boarding facility. Kennel cough is not terribly dangerous in healthy dogs but is bothersome and extremely contagious through the air. It can develop into dangerous pneumonia in older animals.

Signs

Dogs with kennel cough have a dry, hacking cough and often spit out a lot of "foaming gunk." They cough constantly for one to three weeks. Other than that, they seem fine, with a good appetite and zest for life. Most do not even have a fever.

Treatment

Usually no medications are needed, although sometimes a vet will prescribe cough suppressants or antibiotics.

You can prevent kennel cough in your older dog by having him vaccinated with an injectable or intranasal vaccine. Vaccinating is really important if you board your dog or if he visits other dogs in a dog park. Get your older dog vaccinated a few weeks before the boarding date, because it takes a while to build up immunity. Unfortunately, vaccinating with only the commercial kennel cough vaccine (which protects only against the bordetella agent) alone may not completely protect him because of the other infectious agents that are involved with producing the disease. However, most of these other agents (parainfluenza and adenovirus) are part of your dog's routine vaccinations. Unlike most vaccines, the kennel cough vaccine should be given twice a year for the best protection.

Canine Flu

A mysterious respiratory disease has appeared in recent years, first showing up on 14 Greyhound racetracks across the United States and then jumping to the pet population. As with all respiratory problems, flu is most dangerous in senior dogs.

The incubation period is two to five days, and the virus is airborne, spread by sneezing or coughing, by coming into contact with contaminated objects, and even by people moving back and forth between infected and uninfected dogs. The mortality rate for this disease is about 5 percent.

Signs

Not all dogs exposed to the disease develop signs. In fact, nearly 20 percent of infected dogs will display no symptoms at all, becoming "silent shedders" and spreaders of the infection.

For those dogs who do exhibit signs, the most common is a cough that can persist for up to three weeks despite treatment. Some dogs also have a thick nasal discharge that clears up with antibiotics. (This suggests that secondary

Breathing Problems

Dogs with pushed-in faces like Pugs and Pekingese inevitably have more respiratory system problems than dogs with more standard noses like Gordon Setters and Golden Retrievers.

bacterial infections may occur.) More severely affected dogs develop a high fever (from 104° to 106°F [40° to 41.1°C]). A fever is not typical of kennel cough, with which this disease is easily confused.

Treatment

It's important to get your dog vaccinated against kennel cough—in that way, if he starts coughing, you can assume that it's canine flu and seek immediate supportive treatment. Researchers are currently working on a vaccine, but it is not available as of this writing. As with most viral diseases, there's no real treatment, just supportive care.

Pneumonia

Pneumonia is an inflammation of the lungs caused by inhaled material, such as particles of food, and consequent pulmonary dysfunction. In many cases, there is also a bacterial infection. Pneumonia can be acute or chronic. Dogs who are weakened from other diseases are at particular risk.

Signs

Signs include respiratory distress, fever, nasal discharge, and exercise intolerance.

Treatment

Treatment includes oxygen, intravenous fluids, rest, and antibiotics.

SKIN DISORDERS

Skin disease is one of the major reasons that people take their dogs to the vet, possibly because it is so noticeable. The skin is the largest organ in the body and has two layers: the outer epidermis of skin cells and an inner dermis layer that is supported by a layer of fat and very thin muscle. The dermis is made up of a network of connective tissue that also contains nerves, blood vessels, hair follicles, and oil glands.

The skin serves to protect the body from outside invaders, monitor the environment (temperature, etc.), keep moisture in, help to synthesize vitamin D, store nutrients, and release pheromones. Poor skin condition is often the first sign of another disease, such as Cushing's disease, hypothyroidism, or nutritional deficiencies.

Skin Condition

Poor skin condition is often the first sign of another disease, such as Cushing's, hypothyroidism, or nutritional deficiencies.

Lipomas

A lipoma is a soft, rounded, nonpainful fatty mass, usually present just under the skin, although some arise from connective tissue deep between the muscles. Lipomas are extremely common in older dogs, and most are benign, staying in one place and not invading neighboring tissues or

Dogs with pushed-in faces are more prone to respiratory disorders.

metastasizing throughout the body. However, some can become very large. If they occur in a place that is likely to interfere with a dog's movement, they should be removed. Obese animals are most susceptible.

Signs
Look for a soft, painless swelling of any shape or size.

Treatment
Many vets will also take out a lipoma if the dog is undergoing another procedure, because on rare occasions, a lipoma can turn malignant.

Lumps and Bumps
Old dogs get lumpy, and some breeds (like Basset Hounds) get really lumpy. Larger dogs have twice as many soft tissue tumors as the general population of dogs, for some unknown reason.

About 30 percent of all tumors found in dogs and cats occur on the skin, and 20 to 30 percent of them are malignant. Most of the lumps are harmless lipomas, warts, blood blisters (hematomas), or cysts, but don't get too comfortable about any of them.

Signs

It is not often possible to distinguish a cancerous growth from a noncancerous growth by just looking at it. If you find a lump, call your vet.

Treatment

If your vet would like to see your dog, she will probably do what is called a fine needle aspirate to remove some cells from the lump for examination under a microscope. She'll use the same tiny needles that are used for vaccinations, so don't worry about your dog being hurt during the procedure.

In some cases, the vet will want to remove the lump. This is the most likely course of action if:

Use grooming time as an opportunity to inspect your senior for lumps and bumps.

Moderate, controlled exercise is key to your senior's health.

- The lump is malignant.
- The lump is a very large lipoma that interferes with the dog's freedom of movement.
- The lump is a cyst that may rupture and become infected.

URINARY SYSTEM DISORDERS

The urinary system comprises the kidneys, ureters, urinary bladder, and urethra. The system as a whole—and the kidneys in particular—have many important responsibilities in the body. Here are a few:

- produce, transport, store, and excrete urine
- help to regulate blood pressure
- regulate the fluid that surrounds the cells

Senior dogs are prone to bladder and kidney stones.

- regulate the solids in the blood to keep blood concentrations within normal limits

- regulate the acid–base balance by retaining (or eliminating) certain ions in the blood, like sodium, potassium, bicarbonates, and hydroxyl ions

- respond to aldosterone, a hormone produced in the adrenal glands that affects the metabolism of sodium and potassium

- remove waste products, like uric acid and foreign substances detoxified by the liver

- produce hormones that affect red blood cell production

The urinary system generally starts to "give out" as the dog ages, which can lead to a variety of health problems, including bladder and kidney stones, kidney disease and failure, urinary incontinence and inappropriate elimination, urinary tract infections, and weak sphincter.

Bladder and Kidney Stones

Senior dogs are prone to bladder and kidney stones. These are not real "stones" but accumulations of minerals. They can be there for a long time without your noticing any problems, but if they become lodged in the ureter, the duct through which urine is carried from a kidney to the bladder, urine flow can be obstructed, and that's a real problem. Not only will the dog be in great pain, but the backed-up urine can permanently damage the kidneys.

Signs

Some dogs have no signs at all. In other cases, a dog may urinate frequently or have difficult, painful urination. Sometimes there is blood in the urine. The exact signs depend on the location, size, and number of stones.

Treatment

Some kinds of bladder stones can be treated with diet alone, but other types need both surgery and a controlled diet. Your vet will determine the kind of stone, which will then allow her to determine the correct course of treatment.

Signs of renal failure include lack of appetite and lethargy.

Dogs with renal failure need a calm, stress-free environment.

Kidney Disease and Failure

Kidney failure, the "silent killer," affects more than 1 million dogs and cats in the United States every year. The older the dog, the more likely he is to be affected. The most common cause is chronic interstitial nephritis (CIN), a disease with no identified cause. This is the type of kidney disease that most commonly affects dogs older than ten years.

As the kidneys fail, they are increasingly less able to gather up and concentrate toxic waste products from the blood into the urine and to conserve or eliminate water properly. The urine of such dogs is very pale because it has few waste products in it. The dog gradually develops uremic poisoning, which is slow to develop but deadly. Dogs with kidney disease are at increased risk of urinary tract infections as well.

In some cases, kidney disease can be acute, resulting from toxins like antifreeze, blood loss, shock, high blood pressure, leptospirosis, blood clots, and infections. This kind of acute kidney failure is sometimes reversible. An acute case also can lead to a chronic infection; however, chronic disease also can result from nutritional problems; viral, fungal, or bacterial infections; parasites; cancer; amyloidosis (a condition caused by abnormal deposits of a protein in the kidneys); inflammation; autoimmune disease; trauma; breed or genetic predisposition; or most commonly, old age.

Signs

Dogs may not show any signs of renal failure until two-thirds or even three-quarters of kidney function is lost. In fact, the kidneys are so efficient that even failing kidneys can operate for years before signs of disease are apparent, even though they are continuing to deteriorate.

Signs of kidney disease include:

- blood in urine

- diarrhea

- frequent urination (especially at night) or no urination

- increased thirst

- lack of appetite

- lethargy

- pale gums

- poor coat quality

- vomiting

Your vet can perform diagnostic tests to determine if kidney disease is present. Also helpful are a complete blood count and imaging techniques such as X-rays and ultrasound.

Treatment

Your vet may recommend a high-quality diet designed for kidney patients that is moderately restricted in protein, low in phosphorus, and moderately restricted in salt. However, for most older dogs, even those with some kidney failure, recent research shows that reducing dietary protein levels may be unwise—restriction of protein intake does not alter the development of renal lesions, nor does it preserve renal function. Omega-3 fatty acid supplementation and phosphate binders (to keep the level of phosphorus under control)

What are Bladder and Kidney "Stones?"

Bladder and kidney stones are simply accumulations of minerals that can become lodged in the ureter.

may benefit some dogs with chronic renal failure, at least temporarily. Vitamin C and B-complex vitamins as well as anti-ulcer medications can be given as well. Sodium bicarbonate may help to control the changes in the acidity of the blood.

In earlier stages, a dog can get some discomfort relief from IV and subcutaneous fluids, although this is a temporary treatment only, not a cure. His fluid levels need to be maintained to prevent dehydration. One thing that you can do is maintain a calm, stress-free environment for your dog, one that will encourage him to keep drinking and eating normally.

In advanced stages of kidney failure, there are few options. Dialysis is not a good option in chronic renal failure cases except for large dogs with good veins. It must be given several times a week, is extremely expensive, and does not reverse the disease. In fact, by the time the disease is actually diagnosed in dogs, it's usually too far advanced to find measures that will prolong life.

Urinary Incontinence

Urinary incontinence is defined as a loss of voluntary urinary control. It can be caused by a problem in the renal, nervous, or exocrine systems. Never assume that a dog becomes incontinent simply because he is "old" or "senile." There's a reason for everything and a treatment for many things.

Signs

A dog with urinary incontinence is unable to hold his urine and seems to forget his housetraining.

Treatment

Treatment for urinary incontinence depends on the cause. Your vet will diagnose the cause and prescribe the treatment. Various medications are available.

Urinary Tract Infection (UTI)

Urinary tract infections are bacterial infections most common in older, spayed females who have a wider and shorter urethra than males have. In many cases, the problem is that the patient lacks the normal mechanisms to prevent a urinary tract infection. Some dogs have anatomical abnormalities with the vulva or prepuce that allow for urine to be pooled or retained. Some dogs have a misplaced ureter or a neurological problem that won't allow the bladder to empty. Others have an immune system disorder, diabetes, or hyperadrenocorticism. All these conditions can cause a urinary tract infection.

Urinary tract infections can become persistent when a tough

⊰ Senior Moment ⊱

Housetraining Lapses

If your senior dog seems to have forgotten his housetraining, he may be suffering from a medical condition.

To decrease the incidence of urinary tract infections in your senior, give him plenty of fresh clean water.

bacterial infection is not treated long enough with antibiotics. In other cases, the bacteria have found a spot in the urinary tract where they have been protected from attack by the antibiotics. Many so-called recurrent infections are really the same infection that has not been completely destroyed.

Signs
Signs include frequent urination, often with blood.

Treatment
This is a condition easily diagnosed by culturing the urine, although a urinalysis may reveal some telltale bacteria or white blood cells. However, only a real urine culture can identify the organism and so determine what antibiotics should be prescribed.

Here are a few things you can do at home to decrease the incidence of UTIs:

- Give your dog plenty of fresh clean water. If you use dry food, add a little

Glucocorticoids: The New UTI Culprit

Recent research is pointing to a new culprit in urinary tract infections: glucocorticoids (steroids), which are used long term to treat dogs with skin conditions like allergies. Dogs on this therapy have a greater risk of developing UTIs than do dogs who are not so treated, although no one is quite sure why.

Unfortunately, many of these dogs fail to show clinical signs of the problem. Therefore, a regular bacterial culture of urine samples may be necessary to identify UTIs in some dogs receiving long-term glucocorticoid treatment. Failure to recognize and treat UTIs in these dogs may result in serious consequences, such as a severe kidney infection.

liquid or switch to canned food.

- Make sure that your dog gets plenty of walks so that he has an opportunity to urinate frequently (and thus to eliminate bacteria). Dogs who are kept in for long periods and forced to "hold it" are most vulnerable. If you are gone from home for long periods, install a doggy door or hire a dog walker.

Weak Sphincter

Your older dog is housetrained, but sometimes you may find that she (or less commonly, he) has leaked urine during the night. The cause may be the weaker sphincter muscles often found in spayed females, but it turns up occasionally in males and unspayed females as well. The condition affects as many as one-fifth of all female dogs.

Obese dogs are the most frequent sufferers of a weak sphincter. The direct cause is reduced sensitivity of neurological receptors in the sphincter. This means that the dog is not really aware that she needs to go.

A weak sphincter may be mistaken for other problems like diabetes and Cushing's disease, which increase the volume of urine.

Signs

Urinary incontinence is a sign of a weak sphincter.

Treatment

This condition is easy and inexpensive to treat in females. Your veterinarian may prescribe an estrogen supplement. No one is sure why they help, but it is thought they help maintain the neuroreceptors in the bladder's sphincter. Without estrogen (which decreases as females age), the receptors become unresponsive to the transmission of the "storage" message from higher neurological centers.

Another strategy uses "alpha-adrenergic agonists," chemicals taken as pills that facilitate the release of neurotransmitter chemicals that act on the receptors of the sphincter. This helps a dog "hold it."

In male dogs, it is often more difficult to control the trouble. If there is no underlying problem, a combination of testosterone and phenylpropanolamine will often help to control the incontinence. In the cases where this doesn't work, another possibility is a drug that relaxes the muscle fibers of the bladder to help to increase its storage capacity. If all medications fail, there are some surgical options available. After surgery, it's usually best to put the dog on medication, or the incontinence may return. Talk with your vet to see what option will work best for your dog.

Every stage of life, especially the senior stage, seems to have a multitude of diseases that accompany it. This can be scary, but the good news is that nearly every disease can be treated. Even diseases that are not curable can be managed, and that's good news for both you and your senior.

Good preventive care can help to keep your senior dog healthy for years to come.

Chapter 9

THE SUN SETS

It is never easy to talk about the end of life, especially when we are talking about our best doggy friends—or ourselves. Yet sooner or later, the end will come for all of us. Our job is to use the time we have well by providing for our pets' future if we pass first or by helping them pass with grace and dignity should they precede us.

IF YOU GO FIRST

While most of us expect to outlive our pets, the truth is that any of us could get hit by a meteor this afternoon—and where would that leave poor old Fido? In good hands, if you've done your job!

Arranging for the care of your dog in case you pass away first is the responsible thing for any owner, and it takes on additional urgency if you own a senior dog. While a puppy or dog in the prime of his life may find an adopter quickly, the chances are that an older animal, especially if he has a health problem, won't be so lucky. But you can ensure his future comfort long after you're gone.

While England has long looked favorably upon providing for pets after one's demise, things have been a bit slower on this side of the Atlantic. However, in 1990, the National Conference of Commissioners on Uniform State Laws added a section to the Uniform Probate Code to validate "a trust for the care of a designated domestic or pet animal and the animal's offspring." Several states have adopted this section or other legislation with a similar purpose. The best way to arrange all this is to talk with your attorney, who will figure out the best way to carry out your wishes.

Prepare an "Animal Card"

The first step is to prepare an "animal card" for your wallet. If the meteor strikes and you are lying unconscious on the sidewalk, rescue workers will find the card and know that you have a dog at home who needs care while you are in the hospital recovering or dying, as the case may be. The card will contain all the pertinent information about your dog, including a vet contact, health information, and special care. It also should provide a contact for someone who has agreed to take your pet.

The same information should be kept with your important documents in an easily accessible place in your home and at work. Don't risk people "forgetting" about your dog while you are laid up—or laid to rest.

Providing for Your Senior

It has been estimated that more than two-thirds of American pet owners treat their pets as family members—letting them sleep in their beds, buying them Christmas and birthday presents, carrying their photos in their wallets, and even kicking out lovers and spouses who objected to the pet. While this sort of devotion is admirable, it's a sad fact that many people forget to provide for their dog in the event of their own demise. Currently only 15 to 20 percent of people do so. Join their ranks!

Consider a Trust

Your lawyer may suggest that you make a "conditional gift" to your pet's designated caretaker in trust. This makes the actual beneficiary a human being (avoiding some legal tangles). There are different ways to set all this up—let your lawyer advise you. If your lawyer isn't familiar with animal trusts, get one who is.

Select a Caretaker

The main problem for you is to carefully select who will be your dog's caretaker. This is the person who is the technical beneficiary of the trust. You must absolutely trust this person. You also might find it necessary to choose one or more "alternate" caretakers in case your first choice is unavailable when the day comes. Some of those meteors can be quite large.

Age-Defying Tip

If You Can't Set Up a Trust

If you don't have enough money to make a trust a reasonable option, you can simply designate someone you trust very much to care for your animal and will them what you can to help care for the dog. There aren't as many safeguards in this system, but sometimes that is all we can do. You also may consider giving your pet to a rescue organization with a very large donation so that they can find a good home for him or keep him in foster care.

Pick a Trustee

You also will need to pick a trustee, either individual or corporate, who will administer the funds for the benefit of the animal. Your will bequeath the dog to the trustee with directions to deliver the dog to the caretaker (if he's not already there). Don't make the caretaker and the trustee the same person—you can see what might happen.

Set Aside Money for Your Dog

It's important to figure out as nearly as possible how much money will be needed to care for your dog until the end of his days. Monies should include enough for veterinary care, dog boarding, and the like. It's just as dangerous to leave too much money as not enough, though. That encourages other legatees to agitate the courts for some of the money to be transferred to them. (You can get around some of this by writing in your will that anyone who contests it will be cut off completely, but that may not work.) Again, your lawyer is your best friend here.

The trust should clearly define how high on the hog you want your dog to live—and you must provide sufficient money for that lifestyle. For instance, if you want your Poodle professionally trimmed once a month, say so, and provide the money for it. If you want your dog to be on a special or expensive diet, you need to say that as well—and

You can ensure your senior's future comfort long after you're gone.

provide the funds. The trustee should be required to check up on the dog on a regular basis.

Your trust also should declare how the money is to be disbursed to the caretaker: once a month or for reimbursement of expenses, and so on. Some owners wish to provide special monies directly to the caretaker to reimburse her for all the trouble she is going to on behalf of the dog.

The trust also will say where the remainder of the money goes after the pet has passed on. This beneficiary should not be the caretaker for obvious reasons. You could always make the beneficiary a dog-related charity or rescue.

Identify Your Dog Clearly

It's also important to identify your dog clearly. After all, one Weimaraner looks strangely like another, and it might be years before someone catches on to the idea that Sparky could not really be 47 years old and still living happily on the trust fund (with the caretaker continuing to pocket her monthly stipend).

Leave Instructions

Because your dog will eventually die, you need to leave instructions as to how the remains should be handled—such as burial or cremation (and what to do with the ashes). You may want to designate a particular memorial.

THE FADING LIGHT

In most cases, our pets pass away before us. We have longer life spans and have become uncannily good at dodging meteors.

Some people choose hospice for their pets. Others decide on euthanasia when the dog begins to suffer beyond the capacity of medications to relieve it or to improve the quality of life. Still others choose to allow death to come naturally, and when it does, they are present with their dog through all its stages while making him as comfortable as possible. Discuss your options with your veterinarian, who can help you make a wise and ethical choice.

Hospice

Home-based hospice care, offered by some animal hospitals and volunteer groups, is a new movement in veterinary care. The basic idea is to offer comfortable at-home care for a terminally ill pet. It's a wonderful idea, not just for the dog but for his human family, especially children who may be having a hard time coming to terms with the impending death of the family dog. Hospice can help everyone understand the process of dying and in some cases give the dog enough "extra time" to allow distant family members (like kids at college) the chance to come back home and say good-bye.

Euthanasia

If euthanasia is your decision, you will want to talk about which (if any) family members should attend the procedure and what to do with the remains. The fewer surprises at this point, the better.

The actual procedure is simple and painless. It involves giving a large overdose of an intravenous anesthetic that will simply cause your dog to lose consciousness and then pass away quickly and peacefully. You do not have to be present, although some owners wish to be. You also can have your dog heavily sedated or put into a sound sleep first while you say good-bye, and then you can leave. Whatever decision you make will be all right. While it is wonderful if you can be there until the end, if you are hysterical or extremely upset, you may do more harm than good.

Afterward, you may take your dog home for burial or opt for cremation or disposal at the vet's.

GRIEF

Of course you will grieve, but you will do it in your own way, a way that best honors your relationship with your dog. Don't worry about "stages of grief" or other bits of advice that tell you how you should feel and in what order.

Some people wish to donate to a dog rescue in their dog's name. Others write a poem,

SENIOR TALES

"Maggie"

Sarah remembers, "At age 14, my sweet Maggie finally began to fail. She developed a chronic cough brought on by congestive heart failure. My wonderful vet and I discussed our options and decided that Maggie would tell us when it was time to go. Meanwhile, we treated her cough and pampered her every day.

"Finally, two months after her 15th birthday, the medication lost its effectiveness. Maggie was incontinent and coughed constantly, and so I decided to give her the ultimate gift: freedom from her suffering. That day, my gentle old friend slipped quietly from this earth and made her way to a place where she can now see and hear and run and play, free of pain at last."

Your dog may tell you, in his own way, when he's ready to go.

make art or a journal, or find some other way of memorializing their pet. Your grief will be right for you, and so will your healing.

Some people wish to fill their lives immediately with another dog, perhaps deciding to honor their lost friend by saving the life of a doomed cat at the shelter. Other people need more time but know, eventually, that another dog will appear in their lives. What is life without a dog, after all?

Explaining Pet Loss to Children

Explaining death and loss to a young child is difficult. It's also an individual matter that depends on your child's age, your own religious beliefs, and other circumstances. The important thing is to be honest with your child. Children should understand that the dog is not away on a visit or living with another family. They can accept the permanence of death only if you explain it to them. However, if you believe in a life beyond this one, and your religious faith permits, you can certainly comfort your child with the thought that the dog is enjoying a wonderful existence elsewhere, and that she will meet him again. If you do not believe that, you can at least assure your child that the dog is no longer suffering and is at peace.

Young children may regress in development in response to a pet's death, and older ones may become remote or depressed. Encourage your children to talk about their feelings, and don't judge them. Some children even feel guilty, deciding that the pet's death was somehow their fault. Many children believe that if they had done one small thing differently, then everything would be okay. In the rare circumstance that something your child did actually *did* cause the death of a pet, even by accident, I recommend professional counseling. When I was a child, my cousin saw the family dog across the street and called her to come home. The dog obeyed and was hit by an oncoming car and killed. That was a difficult time for all of us.

Resist the urge to go out and get another pet immediately to soothe your child's feelings, even if this is what you would do if you had only yourself to consider. A child

⊰ **Senior Moment** ⊱

Dealing With Grief

Don't be afraid to seek professional help for your grief if you feel overwhelmed by it.

Healing means remembering your beloved dog with tenderness and joy.

might get the wrong message—that pets are commodities to be thrown away when they are used up and replaced with something new and cute. It's also often a good idea to choose a pet that is somewhat different from the first in size and color so that neither of you will be subconsciously comparing the new pet with the old—that's not fair to either.

Helping Your Other Dogs Deal With the Loss

If you have other dogs in your household, they may be affected by the passing of your senior. It's not possible to predict what will happen, however. Many dogs "act out" in various ways and undergo personality or behavior changes. Some are permanent; most are temporary. In many cases, the remaining dog may be reacting more to your grief than to his own. If your remaining dog seems to be suffering from the loss of the senior, try to keep his routine as normal as possible, and give him plenty of attention without overwhelming him.

Adding Another Dog

If you are like most dog owners, you will eventually decide to get another dog. In fact, the more you enjoy your life with your present dog, the more likely it is that you will want to repeat the experience. Some people, in memory of their dog, even go out to the shelter to give another older dog a chance for a happy life.

This is a very personal decision and one that should be made carefully. It's wise to keep a couple of things in mind. First, every dog is unique. You will not be able to "replace" your present dog. Unfortunately, some people feel that the best way to assuage their grief is to pick a dog who appears to be most like the one they just lost: same sex, same breed, same coloring. This is usually a mistake. The second dog is not the first dog, and it would be unfair to expect him to be. If you were so in love with your old dog that you think you can never love another one as much, it's best not to be in a hurry to plunge into the dog owning experience again soon. Give time a chance to work its healing magic, and when that certain pair of yearning dog eyes meet yours, you'll know it's time.

By choosing a dog who is quite different from your first, you'll learn to appreciate him for his own special qualities. If your other dog feared water, maybe you'll choose one who loves a good splash. If your first dog was a jogger, maybe it's time to settle back with a couch potato. Every dog, especially every senior dog, has so much to offer that you really can't go wrong. Just open your heart, and give your new dog a chance.

By choosing a dog who is different from your first, you'll be able to appreciate his own unique qualities.

MEMORIALIZING YOUR DOG

We find many ways to honor the memory of our beloved pets. We recall their names on tombstones, in poetry, and in donations to favorite charities in their name. We plant a tree or even a whole garden in their honor. We display their photos and make scrapbooks. We talk about them with our friends. And we enshrine them forever in our hearts. Our best friend here is time. The hands of the clock are gently healing hands, but healing does not mean "forgotten" or "not missed." Healing means remembering with tenderness and joy.

The sun may have set, but it's been a beautiful day, and for believers, the welcoming darkness has no terrors—only stars. Your dog is one of those stars, and his spirit shines forever, even when a new day has dawned.

❈ *Afterword* ❈

Little in life is more satisfying than owning a dog. Their virtues are legendary: They are loyal, friendly, brave, and cheerful. No one has completely plumbed the mysteries of just why this age-old partnership is so peculiarly and deeply satisfying, but I can guess. People and dogs have been together for tens of thousands of years. They've guarded our sheep, driven our cattle to market, found us our supper, protected our children, led the blind, comforted the sick, fought our wars, and provided us with entertainment and companionship.

Senior dogs in particular are so much like ourselves. We get the same diseases, including arthritis, obesity, diabetes, cancer, and psychiatric problems—most of the gifts of old age and the settled life. Senior dogs have their moods, and they are sensitive to ours. They even experience all the "human" emotions: They get depressed, angry, jealous, scared, bored, and frustrated. They love us devotedly. They are sorry when we are sick.

Your senior dog has lived long enough to know you inside and out. He is part of your life in a way no other creature ever can be—and that includes other humans. He will never lie to you. He prefers your company to that of all beings on earth. He has long ago accepted that your habits are normal. For this alone he deserves some very special attention and pampering—make sure that he gets it!

RESOURCES

Associations and Organizations

Breed Clubs

American Kennel Club (AKC)
5580 Centerview Drive
Raleigh, NC 27606
Telephone: (919) 233-9767
Fax: (919) 233-3627
E-mail: info@akc.org
www.akc.org

Federation Cynologique Internationale (FCI)
Secretariat General de la FCI
Place Albert 1er, 13
B – 6530 Thuin
Belqique
www.fci.be

The Kennel Club
1 Clarges Street
London
W1J 8AB
Telephone: 0870 606 6750
Fax: 0207 518 1058
www.the-kennel-club.org.uk

Pet Sitters

National Association of Professional Pet Sitters
15000 Commerce Parkway, Suite C
Mt. Laurel, New Jersey 08054
Telephone: (856) 439-0324
Fax: (856) 439-0525
E-mail: napps@ahint.com
www.petsitters.org

Pet Sitters International
201 East King Street
King, NC 27021-9161
Telephone: (336) 983-9222
Fax: (336) 983-5266
E-mail: info@petsit.com
www.petsit.com

Rescue Organizations and Animal Welfare Groups

American Humane Association (AHA)
63 Inverness Drive East
Englewood, CO 80112
Telephone: (303) 792-9900
Fax: 792-5333
www.americanhumane.org

American Society for the Prevention of Cruelty to Animals (ASPCA)
424 E. 92nd Street
New York, NY 10128-6804
Telephone: (212) 876-7700
www.aspca.org

Royal Society for the Prevention of Cruelty to Animals (RSPCA)
Telephone: 0870 3335 999
Fax: 0870 7530 284
www.rspca.org.uk

The Humane Society of the United States (HSUS)
2100 L Street, NW
Washington DC 20037
Telephone: (202) 452-1100
www.hsus.org

Therapy

Delta Society
875 124th Ave NE, Suite 101
Bellevue, WA 98005
Telephone: (425) 226-7357
Fax: (425) 235-1076
E-mail: info@deltasociety.org
www.deltasociety.org

Therapy Dogs Incorporated
PO Box 5868
Cheyenne, WY 82003
Telephone: (877) 843-7364
E-mail: therdog@sisna.com
www.therapydogs.com

Therapy Dogs International (TDI)
88 Bartley Road
Flanders, NJ 07836
Telephone: (973) 252-9800
Fax: (973) 252-7171
E-mail: tdi@gti.net
www.tdi-dog.org

Training

Animal Behavior Society
www.animalbehavior.org

Association of Pet Dog Trainers (APDT)
150 Executive Center Drive Box 35
Greenville, SC 29615
Telephone: (800) PET-DOGS
Fax: (864) 331-0767
E-mail: information@apdt.com
www.apdt.com

National Association of Dog
Obedience Instructors (NADOI)
PMB 369
729 Grapevine Hwy.
Hurst, TX 76054-2085
www.nadoi.org

Veterinary and Health Resources

Academy of Veterinary Homeopathy (AVH)
P.O. Box 9280
Wilmington, DE 19809
Telephone: (866) 652-1590
Fax: (866) 652-1590
E-mail: office@TheAVH.org
www.theavh.org

American Animal Hospital Association (AAHA)
P.O. Box 150899
Denver, CO 80215-0899
Telephone: (303) 986-2800
Fax: (303) 986-1700
E-mail: info@aahanet.org
www.aahanet.org/index.cfm

American Holistic Veterinary Medical Association (AHVMA)
2218 Old Emmorton Road
Bel Air, MD 21015
Telephone: (410) 569-0795
Fax: (410) 569-2346
E-mail: office@ahvma.org
www.ahvma.org

American Veterinary Medical Association (AVMA)
1931 North Meacham Road – Suite 100
Schaumburg, IL 60173
Telephone: (847) 925-8070
Fax: (847) 925-1329
E-mail: avmainfo@avma.org
www.avma.org

ASPCA Animal Poison Control Center
1717 South Philo Road, Suite 36
Urbana, IL 61802
Telephone: (888) 426-4435
www.aspca..org

British Veterinary Association (BVA)
7 Mansfield Street
London
W1G 9NQ
Telephone: 020 7636 6541
Fax: 020 7436 2970
E-mail: bvahq@bva.co.uk
www.bva.co.uk

Websites

In Memory of Pets
www.in-memory-of-pets.com

Nylabone
www.nylabone.com

Pet Loss Support Page
www.pet-loss.net

SeniorDogs
www.seniordogs.com

The Senior Dogs Project
www.srdogs.com

INDEX

Note: **Boldfaced** numbers indicate illustrations and tables.

PHOTO CREDITS

DEDICATION

I would like to thank the following people who so generously gave financial support to my favorite dog rescue, Basset Rescue of Old Dominion (BROOD), in honor of their beloved pets. Special thanks go to Sherrilyn Wilson and her BROOD rescue, Jacques, for a major contribution.

Sherrilyn Wilson: Jacques; **Rodica Stoicoiu and Mike Ambrose:** Olivia, Charlotte, Agnes, and Webster; **Frimet Holbrook:** Moose; **Rebecca Moore:** Georgie and Rainy; **Diane McManus:** Hoover; **Marty Selph:** Pollyanna; **Jeannine McElveen:** Ellie and Potomac; **Charlie and Jill Cosgrove:** Louie and Boozer; **Pat LeCates:** Sadie; **Cat Clough:** Winnie and Callie; **Barb Martin:** Tootsie; **Steve and Tracie Van Dorp:** Shannon; **Liz Kielley:** Buford, Daisy Mae, Benzie, Ma Barker, and Dulcie; **Susan Randolph:** Toby and Daisy; **Brian and Karen Parshall:** Coco; **Diane Dalton:** Sheba, Jackson, and Rocky; **Anne Ferguson Rohrer:** Oliver and Caruso; **Andrea Green:** Lily; **Debbie Roberts:** Clarabelle, Roscoe, Casey, Penelope, and Stanley; **Karen Deering:** Winslow and Sherman; **Robin Snell:** Mickey, Nikki, Tina, et al; **April Chang:** JD; **Lisa Wallace:** Humphrey, Hubert, Thumper, and Frankie; **Alison Field:** Sidney; **Anne Prendergast:** Sam; **Buddy and Patty Spangler:** Bea-Bea; **Groves Family:** Riley and Franklin; **Norine Noonan:** Longhorn-Bridi Princess, Live Oak Gretel, and Mitzi; **Ron and Kathie Fuss:** Sammy and Roscoe; **Hugh Seymour:** Dixie and Roy; **Marty Clark:** Roscoe and Sadie; **Jacquelyn Baker:** May; **James Hughes:** Otis, Griff, and Magnum; **Marilyn Brazzle:** All the hounds graduating from the House of Puddles; **Lisa Connors Stratemeyer:** Gracie; **Christine Williams:** Dexter; **Peggy Bartow:** Chelsea; **Therese and Sy Francin:** Sweet Maggie; **Nancy Mattox:** Buddy Lee; **Helen Seldon:** Otis; **Kathi Lockhart:** Harriet and Einstein; **Diane and Bobbye Weatherford:** Penny; **Francin Family:** Reba.

ACKNOWLEDGEMENTS

Thanks to everyone who shared their wisdom and insight with me about the Golden Years of dogs—and as always, special thanks to my wonderful editor Stephanie Fornino at T.F.H. for her care, patience, and unfailing good humor.

ABOUT THE AUTHOR

In her spare time (away from her animals), **Diane Morgan** is an assistant professor of philosophy and religion at Wilson College, Chambersburg, PA. She has written numerous books on canine care and nutrition and has also written many breed books, horse books, and books on Eastern philosophy and religion. She is an avid gardener (and writes about that, too). Diane lives in Williamsport, Maryland, with five dogs—three of whom are seniors and one of whom is 17—two cats, some fish, and a couple of humans.